Easter flower! what would you here?

Easter flower! what would you here?

Anthology of songs and hymns by N.F.S. Grundtvig

Translated into English by John Irons
*in cooperation
with Klaus Høeck*

Selected and edited by
Anne-Marie Mai and
Jørn Henrik Petersen

University Press of Southern Denmark

Easter flower! what would you here?
© John Irons, Klaus Høeck, Anne-Marie Mai and Jørn Henrik Petersen, 2014

Cover: Donald Jensen, Unisats
Cover photo: Polfoto
Layout: Narayana Press
Typeset: Adobe Caslon
Printed by Narayana Press 2014

ISBN: 978 87 7674 717 6

Contents

Introduction	7	Now gleams the sun in all its splendour	57
Lovely is the sky of blue	23	Thrice welcome to the leafy grove	59
Easter flower! what would you here?	25	To rightly bid the world farewell	61
Far higher are mountains in other lands found	29	Is light but for the learned few	63
I know of a land	31	Now every wood grows pale and wan	65
The bright blessed day with joy we see	35	Grey grow the clouds	67
Once more did the dawn cock crow	39	I walked abroad one summer's day	69
Grant me, God, a tongue to praise you	41	Midsummer Night at Frederiksborg	71
If once the Lord's plough you hold sure	43	All birds that God gave wings to fly	73
The church, that ancient house, will stand	45	Golden dawn sees us reborn	75
Hail, you Saviour and Redeemer	47	It's so delightful to be as one	77
It is a wondrous story	49	Ring out, ye bells	79
Lord, of your glory the heavens are telling	51	What sunshine is for the rich black earth	81
Mother's name is a heav'nly sound	53	Danish and English titles	82-83
A simple, cheerful active life on earth	55		

Introduction

Anne-Marie Mai and Jørn Henrik Petersen

There are creative writers and thinkers who are the origin of words or expressions that have a long life in a language. From William Shakespeare's plays, utterances and images have found their way into the English language – and from there into some of the many other languages in the world. Generally speaking, such occurrences are few and far between, since writers of sufficient calibre to leave their distinctive mark on a language are rare, but Danish 19th century literature can boast three such figures: Hans Christian Andersen (1805-1875), Søren Kierkegaard (1813-1855) and Nikolai Frederik Severin Grundtvig (1783-1872), all of whom are still very much present in Danish speech and thought. As far as Hans Christian Andersen is concerned, such words and expressions have also found their way into other languages. 'The Emperor's new clothes' is a well-known expression in English and German, whereas Grundtvig's term 'the living word' is still probably best known in Danish.

It is quite thought-provoking that Andersen, Kierkegaard and Grundtvig were contemporaries. The small, old-fashioned capital of absolutist Denmark, Copenhagen, was in fact the domicile of all three in the mid-19th century. Despite this, they were far from having amicable feelings about each other, let alone feeling mutual admiration. Søren Kierkegaard gave Andersen's first novel a verbal broadside, and he referred to Grundtvig in hardly flattering terms as a home-brewed Norse giant and a yodelling rowdy, while Andersen for his part found Grundtvig conceited and Kierkegaard as heavy as a cobblestone pavement.

Fortunately, skirmishes between the three geniuses no longer disguise the fact that in their separate ways they have all contributed to world literature. Andersen was translated early on – more or less faithfully to the original – and his Fairy Tales told for Children (*Eventyr, fortalt for Børn*) made him world-famous. Søren Kierkegaard's works have long since shown themselves to be indispensable within philosophy, psychology and epistemology, and his works are clearly a *sine qua non* for such 20th century thinkers as Martin Heidegger and Jacques Derrida. Grundtvig is perhaps best known internationally for his modern ideas about lifelong learning and a completely new type of school – the folk high school for young people as well as adults – that was to give people the possibility of developing freely and using their abilities for the benefit of their national community. In the Nordic countries as well as among Nordic emigrants to USA his ideas about popular enlightenment and *dannelse* (for which English often uses the German term *Bildung*) were converted into practical initiatives – and even in India,

South America, Africa and the East his folk high school ideas have lived on after him.

The fact that present-day Denmark is a leading nation within in-service education and liberal adult education is due to Grundtvig's epoch-making ideas about popular enlightenment. So far, however, it is only this corner of Grundtvig's considerable oeuvre that has claimed international attention – in fact, his work includes both pedagogics, theology, linguistics, history, Norse mythology, poetic writing and politics.

The various aspects of his work are interconnected, and even though he produced works – as do practically all writers – that were very much of their age and that now seem completely antiquated, there is inspiration and stimulus to be found for the modern reader when it comes to such concepts as intellectual liberty and a modern society, as well as in his poetic writing, which displays both insight and beauty.

In the present publication, we feature a selection of Grundtvig's well-known hymns and songs. It is precisely in his vast collection of hymns for the Danish church that we find texts that are among the most powerful of his entire work. At their best, his poetic texts have an artistic breadth that can be sensed at once. At the same time, his view of human emancipation, his criticism of everything that is elitist and dogmatic, and his unburdensome and living Christianity permeate the texts. The best way in which we can present Grundtvig internationally today is to show him as a modern writer whose works combine nature, culture and spirit.

Translating hymns and poetic texts from Danish to English is naturally a fearfully difficult task, but our hope is that the selection demonstrates that it is in fact possible – even in such a way that the translations can be used in Grundtvig's tradition: they can and should be sung, not by trained soloists but preferably by an everyday gathering of people who wish to express themselves together about what is most important in human existence: faith, hope and love. In Denmark, community singing still precedes meetings or lectures, punctuates family gatherings, is part of school and church life. Here, Grundtvig's texts have shown themselves to be strong and resilient, and the present English translations – the work of the poet and translator John Irons, in collaboration with the poet Klaus Høeck – will, it is hoped, enhance the pleasure gained from singing them.

Young and in love

Grundtvig was born in 1783 in the small village of Udby in South Zealand, where his father was a traditional clergyman. As a child, Grundtvig was strongly influenced by popular tales, legends, songs and sayings via his old nanny, whom he refers to as a veritable 'Mistress of Language', and he later stressed how important the impulse he then received from the popular idiom was for his entire work.

He left home early in order to prepare himself for studying at Aarhus Katedralskole, passing the final exams there in 1800. He later declared that the school deprived him of any desire to read books, and that he simply slept throughout his time at school. He began to loathe what he referred to as 'the black school', where knowledge and learning were, he felt, nothing but stone-cold rote learning and sterile pedantry. He began to read theology at Copenhagen University and graduated in 1803. His attitude was rationalist, even though he tried to keep up with the Romantic tendencies of the age among the young writers and intellectuals.

In 1805, he became a private tutor at the manor house of Egeløkke on Langeland, where he experienced a violent upheaval of heart and mind when he fell head over heels in love with the lady of the manor, Constance Leth, the mother of the boy he was to teach. All this was as if taken straight out of Goethe's novel *The Sorrows of Young Werther*, which since its publication in 1774 had shaped European fashion. The ill-fated love of a young man for an engaged or married woman was also cultivated in Copenhagen social life, where, for example, Jens Baggesen and Knud Lyne Rahbek experienced emotional storms in true Werther style – without taking their own lives, however. Grundtvig's ill-fated love did not end in a spectacular suicide either, even though he did send the lady of the manor poems that said that his heart would soon turn to ice. In Grundtvig's diary one can follow the emotional chaos resulting from his infatuation, where all the values he has known, and all ideas about his future, disappear. He writes as follows about his new insight:

> I came here. I read the eye of the fair woman, and what were all the books in the world compared to that? What could I ever discover in them that was so dear to me as the sight of her gaze tenderly resting on me? What was reading or speech compared with silently staring at this fair creature? It was the dull lamp compared with the radiant sun.

This impossible love brought him into a state when he 'wandered along dark, untrodden paths, for I had no home'. His love for her tired him out, and he experienced a kind of emptiness that led him to make a definitive break with his own rationalism, university teaching and the pleasant social life of the manor house. He sought for a completely new, greater insight, and found it in a wild fascination with Norse mythology. He discovered what he himself refers to as an entrenchment in Nordic prehistory and early history.

> As long as I can let our ancient history throw up, both inwardly and outwardly, its entrenchment around me, I can live, but if I am torn from this circle, there is nothing to prevent the pursuing Fury from clasping and crushing me in her arms.

The interest in Norse mythology had been growing since the end of the 18th century among young generations of sentimental and pre-Romantic writers in search of patriotic and popular sources to renew culture and literature. Classicism's cultivation of the conceptual and mythical world of Antiquity was abandoned in favour of a fascination with Nordic languages, cultures and myths. So Grundtvig shared his interest in Norse mythology and Nordic languages and history with many other writers, historians and philologists. It was the first modern poet of Danish literature, Johannes Ewald (1743-1781), who had begun on a large scale to produce aesthetic re-interpretations of Norse mythology. For contemporary writers of prose and poetry it was challenging material – a completely new world of motifs that seemed surprising and refreshing when compared with the well-known Greco-Roman mythology that everyone who wrote poetry and drama had been forced to cram into their heads ever since grammar school. Norse mythology was colourful, full of gripping stories, gods, demigods and humans. It was proof that Nordic literature and art had had a magnificent past and beginning. Among other things, Ewald used Norse mythology to portray the conflicts modern man gets caught up in when he claims his independence and insists on his emotions. Adam Oehlenschläger (1779-1850), who at the beginning of the 19th century stood out as an exponent of a completely new national-Romantic style of writing, and who claimed to be Ewald's successor, used the mythology to express allegorically the crisis of contemporary society, where goodness has foundered because citizens are irresponsible and lack culture, and because this results in the disappearance of a cohesive force in society.

Grundtvig, for his part, was out on other business. He attempted to find material in mythology that could renew Christianity. The images of mythology foreshadow the advent of Christianity. Grundtvig places the myths in 'the great struggle for Eternity' – and here the myths function as a natural figurative language – natural because it has emerged out of Nordic popular life and history.

While Grundtvig was licking his wounds after his ill-fated love affair, he seriously got down to studying Old Icelandic and started to gain an overview of Norse mythology, writing that the battle between 'High Odin' and 'White Christ' could be stopped if one viewed both of them as sons of 'The Father of the Universe', God himself. In his poetry he also dealt with how he himself, in the middle of his spiritual crisis, had found God everywhere: in history, in Norse mythology, in nature, in poetry and in the Bible.

His work Mythology of the North (*Nordens Mytologi*, 1808) was a regular polemical treatise as well as a manual that, in narrative prose, communicated the Nordic material in a completely new way, not to experts but to a broader audience. He collected the mythology into a narrative about the powerful Father of the Universe, who leads the world from creation through the final battle of ragnarok to the new heaven. During this phase of his work, he thus links mythology and Christianity in a wild, Romantic construction, and it is not until 1832, in a new version of Mythology of the North, that he places Christianity highest, though without giving up the mythology. Here, on the other hand, he sharpens his thoughts about intellectual liberty in a powerful introductory verse, in which he writes:

Let freedom be our watchword up North,
Freedom for Loki as well as for Thor,
And for the Word in a world that is new [...]

It is typical for Grundtvig not to strive in his poetry for any clear mythological-theological understanding, which he wrestles to bring out in his more academic writings. In his verse, he lets Christian and mythological imagery enter into new constellations without taking strict account of any logic, and it is – among other things – these impulses that are the basis of his Romantic renewal of hymn-writing.

Home to Udby

Grundtvig had escaped from his emotional storm on Langeland and the literary salon genre: soulful infatuation with a married woman. He was busy working on large-scale literary projects and Norse mythology when his father, early in 1810, asked him to return home and become a clergyman. Despite a certain unwillingness, Grundtvig held his probational sermon and had it printed.

This sermon had the title 'How has the word of the Lord disappeared from his house?' and it took the form of a frontal attack on the clergy. Grundtvig felt that the clergy had completely abandoned preaching the gospel and had failed to adopt a stance towards a somnolent age that perhaps wanted to have a religious life, but only if one could yawn one's way to it! His many speculations led to utter exhaustion, and after a long period during which he spent most of his time in lethargy at Valkendorfs Kollegium in Copenhagen, oppressed by his parents' insistence on his return and his own pangs concerning Christianity, he went completely insane. When the breakdown came, Grundtvig's friends managed to get him to his feet, and in a hallucinatory state he was transported home to Udby on 20 December 1810. During a break on the journey, at inns in Rønnede and Vindbyholt, Grundtvig was convinced that he was fighting against the devil himself in the form of a serpent.

In Udby, he gradually recovered from what he himself referred to by the Romantically coloured concept of mental aberration, but for which his father used the more Lutheran term temptation. Later such a state was called manic depression, a state that returned on several occasions during his life, although he managed to survive the condition and in a way make creative use of it in his work.

In 1810, he reconciled himself to the idea of becoming a clergyman, or rather: He began to realise that he could take on the task of renewing the church and religious life. He also came to realise that he could use his Romantic, historical interest to further develop his original interpretation of the connection between Norse mythology and the Christian faith.

The first evidence of him beginning to discover new poetic potential was the song of 'The Three Wise Men' ('Lovely is the sky of blue'), which he wrote between 2 December and 12 December 1810, shortly before his friends got him transported back to Udby (see page 23). 'The Three Wise Men' tells the story of Christ's birth as a colourful tale from the East. One can see from the manuscript how Grundtvig works on the text. The first draft of the song is full of pitch-black Romanticism and the theology of perdition:

We have a bed so broad of girth
This bed it is the great wide earth
Where last rest we'll be taking
Within what is our life's dark night
First past the grave will the swift sight
Of smiling dawn be breaking.

Four-posted is our bed below
From where our gaze must upward go
not be enslaved by sleeping,
The lovely sky above's so blue
So many marvelled at the view
Of golden stars there peeping.

Like a collection of sick creatures, humans lie during their earthly life in a bed, staring out into the dark night while they wait for death! But the words 'lovely' and 'blue' change the mood of the song entirely. And after a number of attempts result in Grundtvig getting the two first lines in place, the rest of the song seems to have come easily: 'Lovely is the sky of blue,/fair it is to gaze on too'. In these simple lines, Grundtvig has managed to bring traditional Christian vocabulary to life.

In his accompanying comments, he underlines that it is in fact a historical hymn, and he argues that it could well be precisely that type of hymn that was needed in the renewal of Christianity. He painted a very dark picture of an age and a Europe that was well on the way to lying 'powerlessly sunken between the gaping abysses of unbelief and superstition and only [able to] drag itself forwards when driven by the iron lashes of despotism, as in the Roman world of old'. In this misery there is no use for more moral elucidations concerning God and Jesus as a paragon of virtue. Both rationalism and the Bildung ethic have failed. Only dramatic, stimulating narratives in the form of bible-related hymns can bring the material to life for its readers. It is also important to show Christ's human aspect. Tales, legends, ballads and chronicles have always made a strong impact on people, Grundtvig claims, and such genres must be made use of in preaching the gospel and in Christian singing. The clergy must learn to tell stories from the Bible about the life of Jesus and to make use of such popular genres as tales and folk songs.

In 1812, Grundtvig's new historical opus World Chronicle (*Verdens Krønike*), his history of the world, in which he made 'God's management of his house' through the ages his main theme. He called his great narrative a historical theodicy that starts with the biblical story of the Creation, after which it ranges very widely, from Luther to Goethe, Rousseau and Oehlenschläger.

Grundtvig rounds off the chronicle by depicting contemporary Europe and the miserable state of the now almost dechristianised Denmark. Here he deals with his own generation's renewed interest in Norse mythology, stating, not without a certain amount of self-criticism, that the Nordic revival has been in danger of going too far. People in Denmark have lost their faith to such an extent that Nordic history and mythology no longer have any quickening effect. In the construction he works with, Norse mythology and Christianity either fit each other too well, or not at all – as Sune Auken points out in the latest major research work on Grundtvig, his doctoral thesis Saga's Mirror: Mythology, History and Christianity in N.F.S. Grundtvig (*Sagas spejl. Mytologi, historie og kristendom hos N.F.S. Grundtvig*) from 2005.

But precisely the song 'The Three Wise Men', which he managed to complete when his crisis and mental illness were at their height, demonstrated that it was possible to bring together the various sources of poetical inspiration in a renewal of both belief and poetry. The song of 'The Three Wise Men' was quite simply a new sort of hymn.

The making of a song collection

After his father's death in 1813, Grundtvig leaves Udby and for a time holds no clerical appointment while he works on translations of sources of Norse mythology. In 1818, he marries and starts a family. In 1821-22, he worked as a clergyman in Præstø, after which he became resident curate at Our Saviour's Church in Copenhagen. It was during these years that Grundtvig launched his strongest attack on the predominantly rationalist theology of the time, and that he made what he himself called incomparable discovery of the living word, passed on through baptism, holy communion and the creed, the confession of faith. He arrives at the idea of the living word around 1824 in the poem New Year's Morning (*Nyaars-Morgen*) in connection with his showdown with rationalist, text-critical theology and with the church authorities' opposition to the popular revival moments and their unauthorised hymn-singing.

According to Grundtvig, the central thing about Christianity is not the written letter of the Bible but the living word, as in the confession of faith at baptism – 'That water-bath in the Word', as he later calls it. If the foundation of Christianity is the living word, passed down through the lives and acts of the congregation, contemporary biblical exegesis with its pointing out that the original, scope and authenticity were highly doubtful was somewhat irrelevant. For Grundtvig, the barb of academic biblical criticism was removed when he shifted his focus from the written language to what is orally passed on in the creed and sacraments. In Grundtvig's conceptual world, the living word has two meanings: The living word refers to personal, oral utterances, and the living word is the word that calls man to life in baptism and holy communion. The crucial thing for Grundtvig is that God and man are linked by a 'word of mouth', spoken by Jesus himself and handed down directly by the interactive Christian community in connection with the confession of faith and the christening ceremony.

The powerful ideas of the living word and the changing congregations through history are further blended with Grundtvig's passionate connection with popular belief and Norse mythology. New Year's Morning forms a distinctive cosmology, one that boldly combines and confronts almost surrealist pictorial material.

In continuation of his discovery of 'the living word', Grundtvig sharply criticised in 1825 the young rationalist professor of theology H.N. Clausen's thesis The Constitution of the Church: The Teaching and Ritual of Catholicism and Protestantism (*Catholicismens og Protestantismens Kirkeforfatning*, 1825). This he did in the publication The Church's Rejoinder to Professor of Theology Dr. H. N. Clausen (*Kirkens Gienmæle mod Professor Theologiæ Dr. H. N. Clausen*, 1825). In it, Grundtvig without further ado declared that Clausen was a false teacher and a seducer of the Christian community. Grundtvig was particularly dissatisfied that Clausen had emphasised that the revelation – i.e. the belief that God has revealed himself in Jesus Christ – was only accessible to humanity via human reason, and in general he found Clausen's ideas highly construed and unworldly. Clausen took no account at all of the long history of the Church and the handing down of tradition.

Grundtvig was condemned for libel for his personal attack on Clausen and for many years was subject to censorship, a ruling that was only repealed in 1837. The conflict between Grundtvig and the church authorities deepened further when, in connection with Whitsun in 1826 and the celebration of the 1000th anniversary of the introduction of Christianity to Denmark, he sought to defy the prohibition laid down by the these authorities against the singing of unauthorised hymns at church services. Among other things, Grundtvig had planned for the hymn 'The bright blessed day' (see page 35), his own version of Hans Thomisøn's day-song of 1569, to be sung in Our Saviour's Church. The bishop regarded 'The bright blessed day' as completely unsuitable and in bad taste, because it compared eternal life in the beyond to life on earth.

What particularly caused offence was the final verse with the line 'Saa reise vi til vort Fædre-Land' where the Danish word 'saa' means 'similarly', 'likewise', i.e. 'Likewise do we journey to our fatherland'. That could then be taken to mean: 'If only life in heaven is just as good as life on earth when at its finest.' The critics claimed that this was how the last verse should be interpreted. This was too much for the church authorities, and Grundtvig was obliged, under protest, to resign from his post. In versions of the text sung nowadays, the word 'saa' is taken to mean 'at a point in time', not as a comparison between two things. The English translation follows this interpretation.

The idea of the living word served as fuel in Grundtvig's fight against rationalist theology, and it was also clear to his adversaries that his view of Christianity would make hymn-singing a central feature of religious life. When the church is no longer to be built of stones, written texts and the authority of the clergy, but of living human beings, of words and the Holy Spirit, as Grundtvig expressed it in his hymn 'The church, that ancient house, will stand' (p. 45), the singing of hymns by the congregation must be given high priority. A number of theologians felt that Grundtvig placed hymn-singing higher than the Bible itself, and viewed this as a sign that he was capable of getting up to absolutely anything!

The story of Grundtvig's song-writing is a long, varied one, and it is difficult to summarise the many movements and changes that take place in his use of biblical, mythological and historical material. But the point is also precisely that the unexpected connections and compilations are what gives the work strength. If one really takes Grundtvig at his word and starts to listen to the poetic language, one is surprised to discover how bold and light his formation of images and the narrative sequence of his poems and hymns actually are. The Whitsun hymn 'Now gleams the sun in all its splendour' (p. 57) allows what is quite simply a sensuous experiencing of an early summer day to develop into a world of images that is both biblical and Romantic. Verse three for example:

And o'er the dust sighs heav'nly breathing,
and through the leaves wind's gently heaving,
and 'neath the clouds a breeze that blew
from paradise is charged anew,
and in the meadow at our feet
from life's own stream comes murmur sweet!

The images follow on each other so simply, and Christian meanings and interpretations come to the fore. The hard struggle with language and thought that Grundtvig could never escape from has here successfully become a figurative language that can be interpreted as being borne by what he himself called a 'pictorial view', i.e. a wordless vision of the spiritual that precisely the poet is able to express in language, over which the spirit itself is master.

Another striking example is the Easter hymn 'Easter flower! what would you here?' (p. 25), where Grundtvig mixes material from Norse mythology into the depiction of Christ's resurrection. It is not immediately obvious, but the mythical material is there, particularly in the following verse:

Easter flower! A drop most strong
from your cup my thirst has sated,
and I quicken before long
wondrously refreshed, elated:
From a swan's song or its wing
it would seem that it did spring.
Now I see the dead reborn in
early flush of Easter Morning.

It is the swan that creates the link between the material from Norse mythology and the Christian mode of thought. Grundtvig takes the swans and the swan's song from the old tale of the two swans that swim to the well of Urd, one of the Fates. For Grundtvig, the swans are an image of the origins of poetry and song, and the connection between Christianity and myths. That is why swan's wings or their song appear in a vision of the Christian resurrection.

Posterity has often mainly considered Grundtvig to be a hymn-writer and a renewer of the church, but apart from that has toned down the Romantic impulse present in his hymn composition. But Grundtvig's hymn-writing can actually be seen as a radicalisation of Romanticism, since his authorship is not rounded off in his hymns but expands into new and bold figurative formations that use the historical narrative, myth, the Christian gospel and poetry in completely original constellations and combinations.

Between 1826 and 1839 Grundtvig held no office, and for part of that time – from 1828 to 1831 – he lived in England, where he studied literature, philology and history. His stay was important for his ideas on a renewal of education and pedagogics, as well as for his recognition of the fact that there was a need to change the absolutist system in Denmark.

In the mid-1830s, Grundtvig began to work purposefully on his major work Song Book for the Danish Church (*Sang-Værk til den danske Kirke*), the first volume of which appeared in 1837. Grundtvig's attempts to renew the hymn genre had to take into account a church culture in which Bishop Balle's Evangelical-Christian Hymn Book (*Evangelisk-kristelig Salmebog*) was authorised, and his Manual of the Evangelical-Christian Religion (*Lærebog i den Evangelisk-Christelige Religion*, 1791) was the basis of clergymen's religious activities and teaching. Even though Balle attempted to restrain the influence of a highly radical rationalist theology, the teaching of virtue had virtually replaced the story of Christ's life and death in his hymn book. The work was strongly influenced by the fact that Balle's hymn book commission did not feel that narratives could be reconciled with the hymn genre. This was precisely Grundtvig's first objection to Balle's hymn book, which he regarded as being neither evangelical nor Christian – indeed, he did not feel it deserved to be called a hymn book at all.

Grundtvig emphasised the narrative element in the hymns about Christ's life and death, as in 'Lovely is the sky of blue'. But resistance to Balle's hymn book and rationalist theology came from various quarters, and when Bishop Mynster and his commission in their draft of a new hymn book in 1843 only included one hymn by Grundtvig, Grundtvig and a growing host of like-minded persons started to publish small booklets of hymns for church festivals and in that way created an alternative to Mynster's authorised edition.

When Grundtvig wrote or rewrote hymns, he partly based his work on his many thoughts about figurative language and a pictorial view, but also on his idea of the seven historical congregations which, in his opinion, had possessed a special spiritual power. The idea of the seven congregations is already present early on in his thinking and it constantly develops during his writing. He arrives at the idea of the seven historical congregations on the basis of his interpretation of the introduction to the Book of Revelation, where St John sends his greetings to seven congregations in the province of Asia. Grundtvig, taking this point in the Bible, then starts to count six congregations which together and in their historical sequence make up the Holy Catholic Church: the Hebrew, the Greek, the Roman, the English, the German and the Nordic, the last of which, Grundtvig believed, was precisely then on its way towards a decisive spiritual renewal of Christianity.

The Nordic congregation's contribution to the seven-pointed star, according to Grundtvig, is an insight into the fact that all mother tongues and mythologies are of importance for Christianity and religious life. Grundtvig also reckoned on the arrival of a seventh congregation, which would be the final one before the Second Coming. He comes to the conclusion that this future congregation will be situated by the River Ganges, i.e. in India.

Grundtvig carefully compiles his Song Book in such a way that texts from all six congregations are included. The book has the great world-historical perspective as its underlying idea, but in itself it hopes to bear witness to the spiritual power of the sixth, the Danish, congregation via his own hymn-writing.

He introduces the work with a long prologue. Here he makes use of an extract from his own New Year's Morning (1824), which depicts his own crises and paths of faith. 'God's peace! wherever you build' is what he also writes here. After this come 146 hymns about the Holy Catholic Church, many of which he has written himself, then 58 Christmas hymns, 117 Easter hymns and 73 Whitsun hymns. The hymns are ordered in such a way that they are modelled on the six congregations, after which Grundtvig concludes with seven original hymns, making a total of 401 hymns. This first part of Song Book for the Danish Church was published as eight booklets, and over the following decade there came new bible-related and spiritual songs, so that the song book eventually comprised around 1,600 hymns. In connection with Grundtvig's 50th anniversary as a clergyman in 1861 he received a large sum of money for a collected edition of the Song Book. Four of his friends took on the assignment and between 1868 and 1881 a total of five volumes was published. The Song Book was reissued in 1944-64 in a six-volume edition and in 1982-84 in a five-volume edition.

Member of parliament

Grundtvig had fought against powerful theological authorities and been subject to censorship, but he also gained considerable recognition and a growing flock of supporters. He published history books, writings about his grand idea of a Nordic folk high school, as well as theological treatises. He also attracted large crowds to his lectures and national meetings, and was elected as a member of the constitutional assembly after the abolition of the absolute monarchy in 1848. There is no collected edition of his writings, but a selection of them accounts for no less than 10 volumes, to which can be added his six-volume song book. A research centre at Aarhus University is working on a collected digital edition of his works.

Twice, Grundtvig was a member of parliament, where he was a staunch opponent of any link between politics and religion. He argued as early as 1827 in a long dissertation in favour of freedom of religion and declared himself to be an opponent of the idea of a state church. His supporters, after the introduction of the constitution in 1849, often met in nonconformist congregations outside the established church of the Folkekirke, but in 1868 'valgmenighedsloven' came into force, an act which made it possible for a minimum of 20 households to form a special congregation outside the Folkekirke. The Grundtvigian congregations of this type were based on his conception of the living word of baptism and the sacrament of holy communion. They distanced themselves from the idea of the clergyman's role as a person of theological authority. Grundtvigian folk high schools and congregations went hand in hand, often organising activities to do with language, literature and history. Expressing oneself through art, culture and history was seen as stressing what was truly human – which made it possible also to have a Christian perspective.

Lectures by dedicated folk high school teachers on art, language and literature sprang from Grundtvig's ideas on the value of each human being and the importance of language. Humanity and Christianity are interconnected, but not in the sense that one only becomes a true human being if one is a Christian. 'Human being first, then Christian' is what Grundtvig wrote in 1837 in a polemical poem that challenged the opposite assertion. For Grundtvig, heathens, Jews, Christians, Moslems and non-believers all have equal value as human beings. Christianity is not some sort of accretion of human Bildung and virtue that makes the Christian person better or more highly developed than the non-believer. Grundtvig later claimed in a sermon in 1867 that the maxim became his slogan, and that he is against a theology which claims that a person must first be destroyed before he or she can become a Christian. Christ was first and foremost the Son of Man.

Grundtvig's way of thinking deprives the clergyman of his authority, but gives both congregation and clergyman important assignments within culture and Bildung. The history of importance of the folk high schools for the youth of rural areas in the 19th and 20th century is also the history of new importance of theologians and clergymen as popular organisers rather than church authorities.

Grundtvig as a social thinker

So far, we have met Grundtvig as a clergyman, poet, politician, theologian, philologist, historian, narrator of myths – and much more besides. He was an epoch-making, boundary-breaking polymath. As such, he also made a contribution as a social thinker. A book has actually recently been published on Grundtvig in a series of 'Political Science Classics' (Ove Korsgaard: *N.F.S. Grundtvig*, 2012), although Grundtvig the political scientist is considerably less known than the hymn-writer, clergyman, narrator of myths, etc. This probably has to do with the fact that he never systematised his 'political theory' – if one can talk of such. His political arguments must be crystallised out of his many publications on school and society, and out of the speeches he gave in The Constitutional National Assembly, the Folketing and the Landsting.

He must firstly be seen as a key figure in the building up of the Danish nation. In Denmark, the nation was rooted in such institutions as the Folkekirke, Folkeskole, folk high school, Folketing, people's parties – in the Danish folk (The Danish word 'folk' = people, nation, race – according to context). Grundtvig made use of his historical studies to categorise 'a Danish folk' as an educational category for those who in the old realm of estates had found themselves on the lower rungs of the social ladder. The primary task of the common people was to view and develop themselves as part of a people (folk), one in which an awareness of estate was replaced by one of a people – a fundamental change of mentality.

The emphasis of the Danish political debate of the 19th century was thus to a greater extent on the concept of the people than on democracy, because 'the people' was an integral part of the struggle against the estates as being that which defined society. Government by the people only became meaningful when a national consciousness, after a long process of Bildung and learning, had completely eradicated the concept of estates. And that was not something that happened overnight.

Grundtvig and the Grundtvigian heritage found expression in the inter-war years when the Social Democratic Party prevented the Nazis from taking out a patent on the concept of 'folk'. With its 1934 party programme Denmark for the people (*Danmark for folket*) the Social Democratic Party wanted to head attempts to build bridges between conflicting groups in the Danish population. The party made a connection between 'the popular', 'the national', 'the social' and 'the democratic' – a reformulation of Grundtvig to fit the conditions of a new age. The prominent Social Democrat Frederik Borgbjerg had said as early as 1933: 'If the Danish people cannot be infected by nazism and fascism, one of the reasons for this can be found in Grundtvig's strong efforts to raise people's awareness of themselves as equal members of a society' – a left-wing Grundtvigian standpoint that was in stark contrast to some of the right-wing Grundtvigians who were then starting to support anti-parliamentary tendencies.

Grundtvig must secondly be viewed as an important source of inspiration behind the Danish understanding of the concept of 'freedom', the key components of which were freedom of religion, civic liberties and personal freedom.

The development of the nation required precisely an end to the mixing of state and religion, church and school. State and school were to be independent of the church. Freedom of religion and a marked liberalisation of church life were alpha and omega for Grundtvig.

A central part of Grundtvig's view of freedom is contained in the opening lines of *Mythology of the North*, cf. above:

Let freedom be our watchword up North,
Freedom for Loki as well as for Thor,
And for the Word in a world that is new [...]

Loki and Thor – two Norse gods with their separate views of the world – are to be seen as an expression of the precarious balance of opposites found in the constant fight between the good and the evil, both of which have a right to a place in life. 'Freedom for Loki as well as for Thor' thus means that a healthy social life can only develop if there is room for both good and evil, truth and lies, life and death. An understanding of the point of this presupposes, then, that it is seen in interaction with personal freedom. The struggle between good and evil reflects the fact that struggle and competition belong to the basic conditions of existence. Grundtvig's freedom is a freedom to duel, with the word as weapon. A language duel is the salt of the community.

This thought was cited by some, in connection with the debate on democracy that came in the wake of the period of occupation (1940-1945), in support of the view that every political view should be allowed to find expression – even when it was undemocratic.

In connection with the concept of freedom, the view of social security is often discussed. Grundtvig is often used and misused here, and one often hears the last part of a verse from 'Far higher are mountains' (p. 29) quoted:

*[…]But every Dane eats of his own daily bread
no matter how humble his dwelling.
And as for great riches, we're on the right track
when few have too much, fewer still suffer lack.*

Many people hear this as being in praise of social equality and a popular community – indeed, they almost use the verse as being in praise of the welfare state. It can of course not be denied that this idea is contained in the verse, but one ought rather to take note of the title of the song 'Far higher are mountains', written shortly after military defeats, national humiliations, a national bankruptcy, and the secession of Norway. The song is perhaps more the expression of the need to make a virtue of necessity. This is an interpretation that gains further credibility when one takes into consideration Grundtvig's dislike of the relief provisions of the 1849 constitution. Any help to the weak should primarily be anchored in the church. Grundtvig is by no means progressive when it comes to social issues.

Even today, Grundtvig continues to play a major role in the political debate, and he is taken to represent highly different views. This reflects the fact that he wrote a great deal and that he said different things at different times. Added to which, he often expressed himself in a mythical language that invites different interpretations. One can clearly identify the Grundtvigian heritage in the left-wing Grundtvigian variant of the Social Democrats and The Social-Liberal Party, while right-wing Grundtvigianism has survived as part of the heritage of Venstre, Denmark's Liberal Party. As he divided people's opinions in the past, so he continues to do in the present.

Grundtvig's final years

On his 70th birthday, Grundtvig was presented with a 'folkegave', a gift from the people, which made it financially possible for him to open a folk high school where his ideas on true education (*Bildung*) could be realised. The school opened in 1856, and he was made a bishop in 1861 in connection with his anniversary of entering the ministry. He married three times, and was the father of five children. His youngest daughter was born in 1860, when Grundtvig was 76 years old. He died peacefully just before his 89th birthday.

Concerning the selection

The present collection of Grundtvig's songs and hymns provides an insight into his universe. In selecting, an attempt has been made to find the best representative texts as well as those that best lend themselves to a good English translation. Not all of Grundtvig's texts are suitable for translation into English, and it has been our aim to create texts that can be used and can be sung. The translations are based on Grundtvig's texts as published in the authorised Danish hymn book (*Den Danske Salmebog* 2002) and Folk High School Song Book (*Højskolesangbogen* 2006). If any other edition is used as source, this is indicated under the Danish text.

The poet and translator John Irons says the following about his work on the translations:

'When translating Grundtvig, I have to take many things into account, some of which are linguistic, others cultural. In trying to strike a chord in English, I have returned to my own upbringing, to the world of English hymns, many of which were products of the mid-19th century, the very time when Grundtvig was writing. The vocabulary of such English hymns is also 'retro' – the words often belong more to the King James Bible of 1611 than to contemporary language. The mood is predominantly Pietist. We have no equivalent to Kingo or Brorson, and many English hymns date from the late 18th and 19th century.

My father was a Methodist local preacher. The founders of Methodism, John and Charles Wesley, produced in the mid-18th century a vast number of singable hymns. In trying to convey the feeling of Grundtvig, I have drawn heavily on the language of the hymns I grew up with.

Grundtvig's hymns not only have a slightly archaic language – they also have to rhyme. But what is rhyme? Danish and English hymn writers differ considerably as to what constitutes a rhyme. Danes tend to assume that a rhyme is a full rhyme, e.g. 'best'/'rest'. English hymn writers, however, will quite happily rhyme 'love'/'move', 'home'/'come' (optical rhyme); 'mourning'/'warning'/'burning', 'sublime'/'Seraphim' (assonantal rhyme), 'farthest'/'harvest', 'tremble'/'temple', (double rhyme with consonantal affinity), 'praise'/'grace' (near rhyme), etc., etc. All the above examples are taken from the Methodist Hymn Book.

So if the translations do not seem to 'rhyme', it is not because the translator cannot do his job. It is because the art of hymn-writing varies from one culture to another.'

We cannot explore every aspect of Grundtvig's poetical world, but it is possible even so to experience his love of intellectual liberty, his zest for life – and particularly ordinary, everyday life where one makes full use of one's abilities. We gain an impression of his theological conceptual world, where the living word is the pivotal idea, and where Christ is the Son of Man, a saviour and redeemer who walks alongside each human being and joins hands with that person, so that together they may enter paradise. The daffodil, a then disdained common flower, is for Grundtvig the most powerful symbol of the resurrection (p. 25). And love between a man and a woman is also praised by Grundtvig, as in his wedding hymn (p. 77), where he writes about the happiness of being able to be together throughout life. His joy in Danish nature during summer when birds are singing and in his native tongue is also evident in many of the texts. His sympathetic understanding of all phases of life is present in his hymn-writing, and he writes passionately about faith, hope and love.

Grundtvig considered the mermaid to be an icon of Denmark, and in his work he used 'mermaid blood' as a symbol of the blending of myth, history and poetic writing. For him, mermaid blood was a primeval poetic substance, and he hoped that there was a dash of it in his songs and hymns.

Selected literature on Grundtvig in English:

Allchin, A. M. 1997: *N.F.S. Grundtvig. An introduction to his life and work*. Publications by The Grundtvig Society, Vol. 27, Aarhus: Aarhus Universitetsforlag.

Alchin, A. M. (ed.) 1993: *Heritage and prophecy. Grundtvig and the English-speaking world*. Publications by The Grundtvig Society, Vol. 24, Aarhus: Aarhus Universitetsforlag.

Auken, S. 2004: 'N. F. S. Grundtvig (1783-1872)'. In M. Stecher-Hansen (ed.), *Danish writers from the Reformation to decadence, 1550-1900*. Detroit, Mich. Bruccoli Clark Layman, Incorporated, pp. 194-212.

Bradley, S. A. J. 2007: N. F. S. Grundtvig: A Life Recalled. An Anthology of Biographical Source-Texts. Publications by The Grundtvig Society, Vol. 37, Aarhus: Aarhus University Press.

Broadbridge, E. (et al. ed.) 2011: *The school for life. N.F.S. Grundtvig on education for the people*, Aarhus: Aarhus Universitetsforlag.

Bugge, Knud Eyvin 1999: *Canada and Grundtvig*, Kroghs Forlag.

Kulich, Jindra 2003: *Grundtvig's educational ideas in Central and Eastern Europe and the Baltic States in the twentieth century*, Copenhagen: Vartov.

Lundgreen-Nielsen, Flemming 1997: 'Grundtvig as a Danish contribution to world culture', *Grundtvig studier*, 1997, pp. 72-101.

Lundgreen-Nielsen, Flemming 1997: 'Grundtvig and Copenhagen during Denmark's golden age', *Meddelelser fra Thorvaldsens Museum*, 1997, pp. 73-95.

Zøllner, Lilian 1994: *Grundtvig's educational ideas in Japan, the Philippines and Israel*, Kroghs Forlag.

Dejlig er den himmel blå

Dejlig er den himmel blå,
lyst det er at se derpå,
hvor de gyldne stjerner blinke,
hvor de smile, hvor de vinke
os fra jorden op til sig,
os fra jorden op til sig.

Det var midt i julenat,
hver en stjerne glimted mat,
men med ét der blev at skue
én så klar på himlens bue
som en lille stjernesol,
som en lille stjernesol.

Når den stjerne lys og blid
sig lod se ved midnatstid,
var det sagn fra gamle dage,
at en konge uden mage
skulle fødes på vor jord,
skulle fødes på vor jord.

Vise mænd fra Østerland
drog i verden ud på stand
for den konge at oplede,
for den konge at tilbede,
som var født i samme stund,
som var født i samme stund.

De ham fandt i Davids hjem,
de ham fandt i Betlehem
uden spir og kongetrone,
der kun sad en fattig kone,
vugged barnet i sit skød,
vugged barnet i sit skød.

Stjernen ledte vise mænd
til vor Herre Kristus hen;
vi har og en ledestjerne,
og når vi den følger gerne,
kommer vi til Jesus Krist,
kommer vi til Jesus Krist.

Denne stjerne lys og mild,
som kan aldrig lede vild,
er hans Guddoms-ord det klare,
som han os lod åbenbare
til at lyse for vor fod,
til at lyse for vor fod.

(1810/1853)

Lovely is the sky of blue

Lovely is the sky of blue,
fair it is to gaze on too,
where the golden stars gleam brightly
where they smile, invite us nightly
to ascend to them on high,
to ascend to them on high.

In the depths of Christmas night
when each star had dimmed its light,
all at once one star amazing
high in heaven's vault was blazing
like a tiny star-like sun,
like a tiny star-like sun.

That this star so soft and bright
showed itself at dead of night
was indeed the legend's sequel
that a king who had no equal
one day would be born on earth,
one day would be born on earth.

Wise men from far Eastern clime
set out without wasting time
for to find this king of story
and adore this king of glory,
born that very midnight hour,
born that very midnight hour.

Bethlehem was where he lay,
there they found him on the hay,
graced with neither crown nor sceptre,
only a poor woman sat there,
rocked the baby in her lap,
rocked the baby in her lap.

'Twas the star the wise men led
to Lord Jesus' lowly bed,
we too have a star to guide us,
if we keep it close beside us,
we will come to Jesus Christ,
we will come to Jesus Christ.

This mild star as bright as day
which can never lead astray
is his holy revelation,
granted as our inspiration,
as a light to guide our feet,
as a light to guide our feet.

(1810/1853)

Påskeblomst! hvad vil du her?

Påskeblomst! hvad vil du her?
Bondeblomst fra landsbyhave
uden duft og pragt og skær!
hvem er du velkommen gave?
Hvem mon, tænker du, har lyst
dig at trykke ømt til bryst?
Mener du, en fugl tør vove
sang om dig i Danmarks skove?

Lever op i sind og hu,
stander op af eders grave,
barnedage! følger nu
med mig ud i faders have!
Lad mig under påskesang,
kirkeklokkens højtidsklang,
blomsten til mit hjerte trykke,
bryst og hoved med den smykke!

Vinterblomst! du melder vår,
fold dig ud i stille kammer!
Ved Guds værk og egne kår
sig kun verdens dåre skammer.
Spottes end din ringe dragt
uden glans og farvepragt,
selv jeg dog på sorten tilje
ligned helst en påskelilje.

Ej i liflig sommerluft
spired du på blomsterstade,
ej så fik du rosens duft,
ikke liljens sølverblade;
under vinterstorm og regn
sprang du frem i golde egn,
ved dit syn kun den sig fryder,
som har kær, hvad du betyder.

Bondeblomst! men er det sandt:
Har du noget at betyde?
Er din prædiken ej tant?
Kan de døde graven bryde?
Stod han op, som ordet går?
Mon hans ord igen opstår?
Springer klart af gule lagen
livet frem med påskedagen?

Kan de døde ej opstå,
intet har vi at betyde,
visne må vi brat i vrå,
ingen have skal vi pryde,
glemmes skal vi under muld,
vil ej vokset underfuld
smelte, støbes i det dunkle
og som lys på graven funkle.

Easter flower! what would you here?

Easter flower! what would you here?
Common flower from village garden,
scentless, lustreless, austere!
Gift that no one e'er would pardon.
Who do you think fain had pressed
such as you to loving breast?
Dare a bird your praise send winging
when in Danish woods it's singing?

Come alive in heart and mind
from your graves now be upstanding,
childhood days! And with me wind
your way out to father's garden!
Let me during Easter song,
church bell's ringing loud and long,
to my heart the flower be pressing
breast and head with it be dressing!

Winter flower! You herald spring,
now unfold in quiet chamber!
Only fools would shame to sing
of God's work, their lot not savour.
Though your humble garb's yet mocked,
dull you are and poorly frocked,
on my bier my wish is fully
to be like an Easter lily.

Not in sweetest summer air
did your roots begin to settle,
nor the rose's scent did share
nor the lily's silver petal.
During winter's storms and rain
you put forth in harsh terrain,
joy alone on hearts to lavish
who your inner meaning cherish.

Common flower! but is it true:
Is your meaning that of waking?
Is your sermon really new?
Can the dead grave's hold be breaking?
Did he rise up, as they claim?
Will his word rise up again?
Does from winding sheet of mourning
life spring forth at Easter's dawning?

If the dead can't rise again,
then our meaning has no substance,
we'll die quickly and in vain,
grace no garden with our presence,
'neath the ground forgotten be
and our wax won't wondrously
melt, be formed in darkest lining
candle-like on graves be shining.

Påskeblomst! En dråbe stærk
drak jeg af dit gule bæger,
og som ved et underværk
den mig hæver, vederkvæger:
Svanevinge, svanesang,
synes mig, af den udsprang.
Vågnende jeg ser de døde
i en påskemorgenrøde.

O, hvor est du mig dog kær,
bondeblomst fra landsbyhave!
Mer end rosen est du værd,
påskeblomst på fædres grave!
Sandt dit budskab er om vår,
om et helligt jubelår,
som hver ædel blomst af døde
skal forklaret igenføde!

Ja, jeg ved, du siger sandt:
Frelseren stod op af døde!
Det er hver langfredags pant
på en påske-morgenrøde:
Hvad er segl og sværd og skjold
mod den Herre kæk og bold?
Avner kun, når han vil ånde,
han, som svor os bod for vånde.

(1817/Bearbejdet 1935)

Easter flower! A drop most strong
from your cup my thirst has sated,
and I quicken before long
wondrously refreshed, elated:
From a swan's song or its wing
it would seem that it did spring.
Now I see the dead reborn in
early flush of Easter Morning

Oh, how dear to me you are,
common flower from village garden!
Dearer than the rose by far,
Easter flower on graves of fathers!
True spring-tidings bringing me,
of a holy jubilee,
as from death each noble flower
you're transfigured at this hour!

Yes, it's true what you allege:
that from death our Saviour's risen
It is each Good Friday's pledge –
Easter Morning bursts death's prison
What are sickle, shield and sword
'Gainst that master brave and bold?
Chaff his breath dispels for certain,
he who swore to bear our burden.

(1817/revised 1935)

Langt højere bjerge så vide på jord

Langt højere bjerge så vide på jord
man har, end hvor bjerg kun er bakke;
men gerne med slette og grønhøj i nord
vi danemænd tage til takke;
vi er ikke skabte til højhed og blæst,
ved jorden at blive, det tjener os bedst.

Langt kønnere egne, vil gerne vi tro,
kan fremmede udenlands finde;
men dansken har hjemme, hvor bøgene gro
ved strand med den fagre kærminde,
og dejligst vi finde, ved vugge og grav,
den blomstrende mark i det bølgende hav.

Langt større bedrifter for ære og sold
måske så man udlænding øve;
omsonst dog ej danemænd førte i skjold
med hjerterne løve ved løve;
lad ørne kun rives om jorderigs bold!
vi bytte ej banner, vi skifte ej skjold.

Langt klogere folk er der sagtens om land
end her mellem bælte og sunde;
til husbehov vi dog har vid og forstand,
vi vil os til guder ej grunde;
og brænder kun hjertet for sandhed og ret,
skal tiden nok vise, vi tænkte ej slet.

Langt højere, ædlere, finere sprog
skal findes på fremmedes tunge;
om højhed og dejlighed danemænd dog
med sandhed kan tale og sjunge;
og træffer vort modersmål ej på et hår,
det smelter dog mere, end fremmedes slår.

Langt mere af malmen så hvid og så rød
fik andre i bjerg og i bytte;
hos dansken dog findes det daglige brød
ej mindre i fattigmands hytte;
og da har i rigdom vi drevet det vidt,
når få har for meget, og færre for lidt.

(1820)

Far higher are mountains in other lands found

Far higher are mountains in other lands found
than here where a hill is thought striking.
But Danes of the North find that grass-covered mounds,
and lowlands are more to their liking.
The lofty and wind-swept may suit all the rest,
to stay down to earth is what serves us Danes best.

Far lovelier, we are prepared to believe,
are foreign climes which we know barely.
But Danes are at home where beech comes into leaf
by shores strewn with fair blue-eyed Mary,
from cradle to grave our most beautiful sight
is fields in full bloom in the waves' glittering light.

Far greater may deeds be for money or fame
by foreigners done, or their scions.
Though never in vain were shields borne by us Danes
with hearts and with three passant lions.
Let eagles for worldly power sharp talons wield!
we'll not change our banner, we'll not trade our shield.

Far cleverer folk may be found anywhere
than where every sound and strait's glinting.
For household use though we have good sense to spare,
we won't make us godlike by thinking.
As long as the heart burns for truth and what's right,
time surely will show that our minds were quite bright.

Far higher, and nobler, and finer the words
that foreigners' lips may be spouting.
Of what's high and lovely can Danes though be heard
to speak and to sing without shouting.
Our native tongue may not strike home to a hair,
but melts the heart more than their tongues cleave
   the air.

Far more of that ore that's so white or so red
did others extract or were selling.
But every Dane eats of his own daily bread
no matter how humble his dwelling.
And as for great riches, we're on the right track
when few have too much, fewer still suffer lack.

(1820)

Jeg kender et land

Jeg kender et land,
hvor håret ej gråner, og tid har ej tand,
hvor solen ej brænder, og bølgen ej slår,
hvor høsten omfavner den blomstrende vår,
hvor aften og morgen går altid i dans
med middagens glans.

O dejlige land,
hvor glasset ej rinder med tårer som sand,
hvor intet man savner, som ønske er værd,
hvor det ikkun fattes, som smertede her!
Hvert menneske søger med længsel i bryst
din smilende kyst.

Forjættede land!
Du hilses i morgenens spejlklare strand,
når barnet mon skue din skygge fuldskøn
og drømmer, du findes, hvor skoven er grøn,
hvor barnet kan dele med blomster og siv
sit smil og sit liv.

O flygtige drøm
om eviglieds-øen i tidernes strøm,
om templet for glæden i tårernes dal,
om halvgudelivet i dødningesal!
Med dig fra de fleste henfarer på stand
de levendes land.

O skuffende drøm!
Du skinnende boble på tidernes strøm!
Forgæves dig skjalden med mund og med pen
af glimrende skygger vil skabe igen.
Når skyggen er ligest, da hulker de små,
som stirrer derpå.

Fortryllende drøm
om eviglieds-perlen i tidernes strøm!
Du gækker de arme, der søger omsonst,
hvad hjertet begærer, i billed og kunst,
så varigst de kalder, hvad sikkert forgår
som timer og år.

O kærligheds Ånd!
Lad barnlig mig kysse din strålende hånd,
som rækker fra Himlen til jorderigs muld
og rører vort øje med fingre som guld,
så blålig sig hæver bag buldrende strand
det dejlige land!

O himmelske navn,
som åbner for vores din hellige favn,
så Ånden, usmittet, kan røre ved støv
og levendegøre det visnede løv!
O, lad mig nedknæle så dybt i mit ler,
at Gud mig kun ser!

I know of a land

I know of a land
Where hair does not grey, and where time's rule
    is banned,
Where sun does not burn, and where wave does
    not ring,
Where autumn embraces the blossoming spring,
Where morning and evening unceasingly dance
In noon's brightest glance.

Oh, wonderful land,
Where glass does not run full of tear-drops as sand,
Where nothing is wanting that's worth holding dear,
Where that does not lack which so pained us
    back here!
With breast filled with longing we seek ever more
Your sweet-smiling shore.

Oh, long-promised land!
We greet you in morning hour's mirror-clear strand,
When perfect your shadow the child may espy
And where woods are green dreams that there
    you must lie,
Where too it can share with the rushes and flowers
Its smile and its hours.

Oh, transient dream
Of island eternal in time's rushing stream!
Of joy's sacred temple in life's vale of tears,
Of life half-divine in this hall's mortal years!
The land of the living with you melts away
From those made of clay.

Oh, hope-dashing dream!
You glittering bubble on time's rushing stream!
In vain would the poet, with voice and with pen,
From bright-gleaming shadows create you again;
Where shadow comes closest, the small will all weep
Who on it gaze deep.

Oh, spell-binding dream
Of pearl that's eternal in time's rushing stream!
You fool those poor persons who all seek in vain
In image and art what the heart would retain,
And make them call lasting what just disappears
Like days, months and years.

Oh, spirit of love!
Your hand let me kiss, reaching down from above
From heaven's fair skies to this earth's murky hold
And touching our eyes with its fingers of gold,
So blue-tinged there climbs behind surf-roaring strand
The wonderful land!

Oh, heavenly name,
Whose sacred embrace does our nature enflame,
So spirit can mingle with dust without grief
And bring back to life every dead withered leaf!
Oh, deep in my clay let me fall on my knee
So God may see me!

O vidunder-tro,
som slår over dybet den hvælvede bro,
der isgangen trodser i buldrende strand
fra dødningehjem til de levendes land!
Sid lavere hos mig, du højbårne gæst,
det huer dig bedst!

Letvingede håb!
Gudbroder, genfødt i den hellige dåb!
For rejserne mange til landet bag hav,
for tidender gode, for trøsten, du gav,
lad så mig dig takke, at glæde jeg ser,
når håb er ej mer!

O kærlighed selv,
du rolige kilde for kræfternes elv!
Han kalder dig Fader, som løser vort bånd,
al livskraft i sjælen er gnist af din Ånd,
dit rige er der, hvor man død byder trods,
det komme til os!

Vor Fader så huld!
Du gerne vil trone i templet af muld,
som Ånden opbygger i Midlerens navn,
med rygende alter i menneskefavn,
med himmellys-bolig af gnisten i løn
til dig og din Søn.

O kristelighed!
Du skænker vort hjerte, hvad verden ej ved,
hvad svagt vi kun skimter, mens øjet er blåt,
det lever dog i os, det føler vi godt:
Mit land, siger Livet, er Himmel og jord,
hvor kærlighed bor.

(1824)

Oh, faith beyond bliss,
Whose high-vaulted bridge spans the gaping abyss
When drifting ice threatens in surf-roaring strand
From poor mortal dwelling to far promised land!
Come farther down to me, you high-honoured guest!
That pleases you best.

Oh, hope fleet of wing!
Oh, brother reborn through divine christening!
For all journeys made to the land o'er the sea,
Good tidings and comfort you've lavished on me,
May I ever thank you, so joy is in store
When hope is no more!

Oh, love perfect love!
Quiet source of fierce torrents that mightily move!
He calls you his father who ransoms our plight
Your spirit all soul's vital force does ignite;
Your kingdom is there where man death does defy;
May us it be nigh!

Our father sublime!
You willingly reign in earth's temple of grime,
Who builds up the spirit in Jesus' sweet name,
In human embrace with an altar aflame,
With heaven-bright dwelling of faith dearly won,
For you and your son.

Oh, Christian faith sweet!
You grant every heart what the world cannot greet;
What barely we glimpse while our eye is still blue,
Is living within us, we know this is true;
Both heaven and earth are my land, life confides
Where love e'er resides.

(1824)

Den signede dag med fryd vi ser

Den signede dag med fryd vi ser
af havet til os opkomme;
den lyse på himlen mer og mer,
os alle til lyst og fromme!
Det kendes på os som lysets børn,
at natten hun er nu omme!

Den signede stund, den midnatstid,
vor Herre han lod sig føde,
da klared det op i østerlid
til dejligste morgenrøde;
da lyset oprandt, som jordens bold
skal lysne udi og gløde.

Om levende blev hvert træ i skov,
og var så hvert blad en tunge,
de kunne dog ej Guds nådes lov
med værdelig røst udsjunge;
thi evig nu skinner livets lys
for gamle og så for unge.

Ja, havde end mål hvert strå i vang,
hver urt udi mark og lunde,
slet ikke for os den takke-sang
opstemme til gavns de kunne,
som dagen hør til, for lys og liv,
mens tusinde år henrunde.

Forgæves det er, med liden magt,
at ville mod bjerg opspringe;
men ørnen er snild, han når sin agt,
når vejret ham bær på vinge;
og lærken hun er en lille fugl,
kan lystig i sky sig svinge.

Med sus og med brus den stride å
nedsuser fra klippe-tinde,
ej mæle så lydt de bække små,
dog risle de fort og rinde;
så frydelig sno de sig fra eng
op under de grønne linde!

Så takke vi Gud, vor Fader god,
som lærken i morgenrøde,
for dagen, han os oprinde lod,
for livet, han gav af døde,
for alt, hvad på mark, i tusind år,
der groed til sjæle-føde.

Så længe vi se den gyldne sol,
og skoven er daners have,
da plante vi maj i kirkestol
og blomster på fædres grave,
til glædelig fest med liv og lyst,
til mindelig pinse-gave!

The bright blessed day with joy we see

The bright blessed day with joy we see
Rise out of the sea at dawning;
It lightens the sky unceasingly,
Our gain and delight adorning!
As children of light we sense that soon
Dark night will give way to morning!

Our Lord chose the blessed midnight hour
To come down without our knowing,
Then clear in the east in dawn's pale bower
The sun's hues in strength were growing:
Then light filled the sky, in which the earth
Shall shimmer with inner glowing!

Were each forest tree to come alive,
And each leaf a voice be granted,
The law of God's mercy they'd contrive
In vain in words to have chanted;
Since life's light now shines for ever more,
In old and young firmly planted!

Yea, though every blade of grass could speak,
In meadow or field or clearing,
A thanksgiving hymn they could not seek
To sing for our human hearing,
Befitting the day, for light and life,
While eons their course are steering.

In vain would the weak man try who chose
To conquer the mountain summit,
The eagle is wily, though, and knows
The wind will not let it plummet,
And even the small blithe lark can brave
The sky and yet overcome it.

The river so brash with thund'rous noise
From crag-face comes downwards crashing
The streams down below have no such voice,
Though murmur with gentle plashing,
So gently they wind through grassy lea
Up under the lime trees splashing!

So thank we our God, our father good,
As larks in their dawn-time chorus,
For each day he gave, as so we should
For life he from death won for us,
For all that has nurtured human souls
For thousands of years before us!

As long as we see the golden day,
And woods are the Danes' own bowers,
We'll deck every pew with sprigs of may
And forefathers' graves with flowers
A wonderful feast of life and joy,
A Whitsuntide gift that's ours!

Da rinde vel og, som bække små,
fra øjne os tårer milde,
og bække i flok de gør en å,
den higer mod lysets kilde,
den stiger i løn, som hjertesuk,
alt årle, og dog end silde.

Som aldrig så lang er nogen dag,
at aften er jo i vente,
så haver det lys og solbjærgs-lag,
som Gud udi kirken tændte;
men immer det dages dog på ny,
hvor hjerterne morgen vente!

Nu sagtelig skrid, du pinsedag,
med stråler i krans om tinde!
hver time til Herrens velbehag
som bækken i eng henrinde,
så frydelig sig den sidste snoer
op under de grønne linde.

Som guld er den årle morgenstund,
når dagen opstår af døde,
dog kysser os og med guld i mund
den liflige aftenrøde,
så tindre end må det matte blik,
de blegnede kinder gløde.

Så rejse vi til vort fædreland,
dér ligger ej dag i dvale,
dér stander en borg så prud og grand
med gammen i gyldne sale,
så frydelig der til evig tid
med venner i lys vi tale!

(1826/1846)

Tekstforlæg:
"Den signede Dag med Fryd vi seer", *Grundtvigs Sangværk*, bd. III, Det danske Forlag, 1948, s. 161ff. Retskrivningen er moderniseret.

And then from our eyes will start to flow
Mild tears like a stream now thriving,
And streams join and to a river grow
That fain for Life's Source is striving
It secretly gains, like some deep sigh,
So early yet late arriving!

And no day can have so long a growth
That evening cannot be sighted,
Its light and its setting sun are both
What God in his church has lighted;
But ever again it dawns anew
For hearts who in morn delighted!

Let day gently glide this Whitsuntide,
With haloing rays full-flashing!
The hours pleasing God as past they slide,
As meadowland stream soft-plashing,
So joyously now the last one winds,
Up under the lime trees splashing!

Like gold is the dawn just moments old,
When day from its death is rising,
Yet we too are kissed with lips of gold
By sunset so sweet-enticing,
Then every dull gaze will glint afresh,
Pale cheeks with new blush surprising!

We'll journey then to our fatherland,
Where no day lies still thereafter,
Where stands a strong castle, proud and grand,
Whose halls all resound with laughter,
And there we will talk till time is done
In light with our friends hereafter!

(1826/1846)

Morgenhanen atter gol

Morgenhanen atter gol,
slog med dugget vinge,
lykke os den gyldne sol
vil med lyset bringe,
når vi takke ham i løn,
over alle sole,
som gør morgenrøden skøn,
signer livets skole.

Dagen har han skabt til dåd,
skumringen til hvile,
ingen målte livets tråd,
derfor lad os ile:
gøre gavn, mens dagen går,
prøve vore kræfter,
visse på, at gode kår
rette sig derefter!

Ord i mund og skrift i bog
skal vor ungdom lære:
ret at bruge kraft og sprog,
livet til Guds ære;
da vor manddom, klog og stærk,
svare skal til navnet,
krone skolens ungdomsværk,
vise, det har gavnet.

(1833)

Once more did the dawn cock crow

Once more did the dawn cock crow,
flapped its wing, dew-clinging –
joy the golden sun will show,
with the light be bringing,
when in secret Him we praise,
though all suns confessing,
who has made such beauteous days,
life's school we are blessing.

Days for action he has made,
eventide for resting,
no one knows when life will fade,
no time let's be wasting:
be of use while day shines bright,
all our strength be showing,
sure that what then comes aright
from its source is flowing!

Spoken word and printed page
teach our youth life's story,
so it power and tongue engage,
life too, to God's glory:
then our manhood, strong and wise
its fine name will merit,
be the school of life's great prize,
its great boon inherit.

(1833)

Giv mig, Gud, en salmetunge

Giv mig, Gud, en salmetunge,
så for dig jeg ret kan sjunge
højt og lydelig,
så jeg føle kan med glæde,
sødt det er om dig at kvæde
uden skrømt og svig!

Himlene din glans forkynde,
lad hver morgen mig begynde
dagen med din pris!
Og når aftenklokken ringer,
lad min sang på lærkevinger
stige ligervis!

Aldrig noksom dig kan love
mand på mark og fugl i skove
for din miskundhed;
lige god i ny og næde,
gør du, os til gavn og glæde,
mer end engle ved.

Hvert dit værk er stort vidunder,
i din visdom ingen bunder,
som af den har øst.
Kun en dåre tør det nægte,
at hos dig er alting ægte,
alting mageløst.

Græsset lig er hver en synder,
ender, før han ret begynder,
visner i sin vår;
himle selv forgå af ælde,
men i grundfast guddomsvælde
evig du består.

Dine fjender gå til grunde,
ja, som avner skal de onde
hvirvles, vejres hen,
mens i alderdommens dage
herlig kræfterne tiltage
hos din gode ven.

Se! fra dine drivehuse
i det fri, hvor storme suse,
poder plantes ud!
Og når de som sne er hvide,
finest frugt om vintertide
bære de for Gud.

Om end gennem dage hårde,
blomstre skal i dine gårde
hvert et hjerteskud,
bære frugt på gamle dage,
medens bjerg og skov gentage:
Ejegod er Gud!

(1836/1868)

Grant me, God, a tongue to praise you

Grant me, God, a tongue to praise you,
that resoundingly displays you
with a psalmist's art,
so that I may feel with gladness
he who lauds you knows no sadness,
has an upright heart!

Heav'n your glory is proclaiming,
may I too in praise be naming
you when day is nigh!
And when evening bells are ringing
may my song like larks be winging
through the twilight sky!

There's no man or beast whatever
for your loving kindness ever
ample praise can show,
you to us in joy and sorrow
give both now as on the morrow
more than angels know.

At your marvels we but wonder,
at your wisdom all must ponder
who have had full share.
Only fools seek to conceal
everything with you is real
and beyond compare.

As the grass is every sinner,
ends while he is but beginner,
fades while yet it's spring;
even heavens are time's minion,
but in your divine dominion
you are always King.

All your foes will soon be shattered,
yea, as chaff they will be scattered
to earth's farthest end,
while old age will without ceasing
witness wondrous powers increasing
with your trusted friend.

See, from your great forcing houses,
outdoors where the storm carouses,
planted shoots take root!
And, when white as snow appearing,
they will for their Lord be bearing
all their winter fruit.

Even though the days be dour,
in your orchards there will flower
every shoot and bud,
in old age their fruit be bearing,
with the hills and woods declaring:
God is wise and good!

(1836/1868)

Har hånd du lagt på Herrens plov

Har hånd du lagt på Herrens plov,
da se dig ej tilbage!
Se ej til verdens trylleskov
og ej til Sodoms plage!
men pløj din fure, strø Guds sæd!
er jorden dig for tør, så græd!
vil gråden kvæle røsten,
så tænk på gyldenhøsten!

Men sker det end, du ser dig om,
for vi er alle svage,
på stand dit kald dog ihukom,
gør ej et skridt tilbage!
Tilbage vender livet ej,
al krebsegang er kun dødens vej;
om hastværk fald dig bragte,
så lær kun at gå sagte!

Så fremad da i Jesu navn,
trods stene og trods stokke!
Og stands ej, om end lue-favn
dig byder stolte blokke!
På gløder går vi allen stund,
hvad skin end har den falske grund;
hvi ej engang i lue,
hvor alt er klart til skue!

Det er jo kun en liden stund,
så er vort løb til ende,
og døden er jo kun et blund,
som vi fra søvnen kende,
og hvilen er den fred, vi nød
vi véd, er mer end møjen sød;
og daglig vi jo kvæde:
Gid evig var vor glæde!

(1836)

Tekstforlæg:
Folkehøjskolens sangbog, 15. udgave, 1969, s. 235ff.

If once the Lord's plough you hold sure

If once the Lord's plough you hold sure,
Cast not a glance behind you!
The world's enchanted wood ignore,
Ne'er Sodom's plague let bind you;
But plough your furrow, sow God's seed!
And if the earth's too dry, then weep!
Though tears your voice may thicken,
The golden harvest beckons!

And should you cast a backward glance,
Through frailty all forsaking,
Think of your calling, hold your stance,
No rearward step be taking!
For one life only you have breath,
Each scuttling move's the path of death!
Should haste hard falls have brought you,
May patience they have taught you!

Then onward go in Jesus' name,
Though sticks and stones impede you!
And pause not, e'en embraced by flames
That boulder-like now meet you!
We walk on coals where'er we go
Whate'er the ground might falsely show,
'Tis not the fire where really
We'll one day see things clearly!

But briefly will our life here last,
Our days are few in number,
A merest nap and death is past
As if 'twere earthly slumber,
The peace in rest that we enjoyed
Is sweeter than the toil employed;
Our pious wish diurnal:
Were but our joy eternal!

(1836)

Kirken den er et gammelt hus

Kirken den er et gammelt hus,
står, om end tårnene falde;
tårne fuldmange sank i grus,
klokker end kime og kalde,
kalde på gammel og på ung,
mest dog på sjælen træt og tung,
syg for den evige hvile.

Himlenes Gud vist ej bebor
huse, som hænder mon bygge,
arke-paulunet var på jord
kun af hans tempel en skygge;
dog sig en bolig underfuld
bygged han selv af støv og muld,
rejste af gruset i nåde.

Vi er Guds hus og kirke nu,
bygget af levende stene,
som under kors med ærlig hu
troen og dåben forene;
var vi på jord ej mer end to,
bygge dog ville han og bo
hos os i hele sin vælde.

Samles vi kan da med vor drot
selv i den laveste hytte,
finde med Peder: her er godt!
tog ej al verden i bytte;
nær som sit ord i allen stund
er han vort hjerte og vor mund,
drot over tiden og rummet.

Husene dog med kirkenavn,
bygget til Frelserens ære,
hvor han de små tog tit i favn,
er os som hjemmet så kære;
dejlige ting i dem er sagt,
sluttet har der med os sin pagt
han, som os Himmerig skænker.

Fonten os minder om vor dåb,
altret om nadverens nåde,
alt med Guds ord om tro og håb
og om Guds kærligheds gåde,
huset om ham, hvis ord består,
Kristus, i dag alt som i går,
evig Guds Søn, vor genløser.

Give da Gud, at hvor vi bo,
altid, når klokkerne ringe,
folket forsamles i Jesu tro
der, hvor det plejed at klinge:
Verden vel ej, men I mig ser,
alt, hvad jeg siger, se, det sker;
fred være med eder alle!

(1836/1853)

The church, that ancient house, will stand

The church, that ancient house, will stand
though its towers may keep on falling,
many lie ruined, deep in sand,
yet their bells still go on calling,
calling the young as well as old,
mostly to those with wearied soul
whose longing is rest eternal.

No house that human hands have raised
can be the Lord our God's temple,
the tabernacle can, though praised,
but as shadow it resemble.
Yet God a wondrous dwelling made,
formed it from merely earthly clay,
raised it from dust by his mercy.

We are his house and church, a shrine
built out of stones that are living,
who, 'neath the cross, baptism combine
with faith in heartfelt thanksgiving.
Were we but two or three, e'en so
he'd choose to build and dwell below
amongst us in all his glory.

We with our king can meet and pray
in the humblest hut if need be,
can say with Peter: Here I'd stay,
though the world were offered freely;
close as his word, he'll ne'er depart,
he is our mouth, likewise our heart,
o'er time and space king and ruler.

Houses which churches have as name,
built all in praise of our Saviour,
where to his arms oft children came,
as home we cherish and savour.
Wonderful things are spoken there,
the pact concluded that we share
with him who grants us all heaven.

The font baptism calls to mind,
the altar joys of communion,
God's word where faith and hope combine
with his love in mystic union,
the house of God, whose word endures,
Christ, who eternal life ensures,
God's living Son, our Redeemer.

May then God grant, where'er our home,
always when church bells are pealing,
people in Christian faith will come
to where they can hear when kneeling:
Not as the world sees, you see me,
all that I say will come to be,
my peace I leave with you always!

(1836/1853)

Hil dig, Frelser og Forsoner

Hil dig, Frelser og Forsoner!
Verden dig med torne kroner,
du det ser, jeg har i sinde
rosenkrans om kors at vinde,
giv dertil mig mod og held!

Hvad har dig hos Gud bedrøvet,
og hvad elsked du hos støvet,
at du ville alt opgive
for at holde os i live,
os dig at meddele hel?

Kærligheden, hjertegløden
stærkere var her end døden;
heller giver du end tager,
ene derfor dig behager
korsets død i vores sted.

Ak! nu føler jeg til fulde
hjertets hårdhed, hjertets kulde.
Hvad udsprang af disse fjelde,
navnet værd, til at gengælde,
Frelsermand, din kærlighed?

Dog jeg tror, af dine vunder
væld udsprang til stort vidunder,
mægtigt til hver sten at vælte,
til isbjerge selv at smelte,
til at tvætte hjertet rent.

Derfor beder jeg med tårer:
Led den ind i mine årer,
floden, som kan klipper vælte,
floden, som kan isbjerg smelte,
som kan blodskyld tvætte af!

Du, som har dig selv mig givet,
lad i dig mig elske livet,
så for dig kun hjertet banker,
så kun du i mine tanker
er den dybe sammenhæng!

Skønt jeg må som blomsten visne,
skønt min hånd og barm må isne,
du, jeg tror, kan det så mage,
at jeg døden ej skal smage,
du betalte syndens sold.

Ja, jeg tror på korsets gåde,
gør det, Frelser, af din nåde.
Stå mig bi, når fjenden frister!
Ræk mig hånd, når øjet brister!
Sig: vi går til Paradis!

(1837)

Hail, you Saviour and Redeemer

Hail, you Saviour and Redeemer,
crowned with thorns by the blasphemer,
you know well, my cross when seeking
I rose garlands would be weaving,
grant me courage and success!

What in God was there to grieve you,
what in dust to love or please you,
that, all your divineness waiving,
you mankind must needs be saving,
and be fully known to us?

Here were love and heart most fervent
mightier than death, their servant;
less for taking than for giving,
solely therefore you were willing
on the cross to take our place!

Ah! I savour now the wholeness
of heart's hardness, of heart's coldness!
What could rise from rocks unswaying,
worthy, able of repaying,
my Redeemer, your great love?

From your wounds, though, a great river
rose that can mankind deliver,
with such power each rock to tumble,
even icebergs cause to crumble,
and to wash the heart quite pure!

Therefore tearfully I'm praying:
Fill my veins without delaying
with that spring that makes rocks tumble,
that can make the iceberg crumble,
and our blood guilt wash away!

You, who me yourself have given,
let me love life, by you driven,
so my heart beats only for you,
so you in my thoughts ensure you
e'er their deepest meaning be.

Though like flowers I too must wither,
hand and breast must ice-cold shiver,
you'll not let me taste death's anguish,
you in sin won't let me languish,
for its wages you have paid!

In your cross I trust completely,
Saviour, by your mercy heed me.
Help me when my foes travail me!
take my hand, when death assails me!
say: We go to Paradise!

(1837)

Forunderligt at sige

Forunderligt at sige
og sært at tænke på,
at kongen til Guds rige
i stalden fødes må,
at himlens lys og ære,
det levende Guds Ord,
skal husvild blandt os være,
som armods søn på jord!

Selv spurven har sin rede,
kan bygge dér og bo,
en svale ej tør lede
om nattely og ro;
de vilde dyr i hule
har hver sin egen vrå,
skal sig min Frelser skjule
i fremmed stald på strå?

Nej, kom, jeg vil oplukke
mit hjerte, sjæl og sind,
ja, bede, synge, sukke:
Kom, Jesus, kom herind!
Det er ej fremmed bolig,
du den har dyre købt!
Her skal du hvile rolig
i kærligheden svøbt.

(1837)

Tekstforlæg:
Folkehøjskolens sangbog, 15. udgave, 1969, s. 142 ff.

It is a wondrous story

It is a wondrous story
and strange if pondered deep
that God's realm's future glory
must in a manger sleep,
that heaven's light and splendour,
the living word for sure,
shall homeless 'mongst us wander
as poorest of the poor!

A nest has e'en the sparrow
where it can build a home,
nor needs the fleeting swallow
for night-time shelter roam.
The beasts need know no anguish,
in caves there's rest in store,-
Shall then my Saviour languish
upon some stable's straw?

No, come, I will throw open
my heart, my soul and mind,
yes, sing, sigh, prayers have spoken,
Come, Jesus, come and find!
It is no unknown chamber,
you bought it with your blood!
Here will you sweetly slumber
in love now swathed for good.

(1837)

Himlene, Herre, fortælle din ære

Himlene, Herre, fortælle din ære,
Mesteren prises af hvælvingen blå,
solen og månen og stjernernes hære
vise os, hvad dine hænder formå.

Men i dit hus, i din kirke på jorden,
der tale dage med dage om dig,
der sig forklarer din sol og din torden,
der på oplysning selv natten er rig.

Ej er i sandhed der ord eller tanke,
som i dit hus jo fik mæle og røst,
og alt så vide, som stjernerne vanke,
bringe på jord de oplysning og trøst.

Ordet med solen i skiftende tider
udgår som brudgom i morgenrød glans,
strålende frem ad sin bane det skrider,
krones som helten med aftenrød krans.

Så på sin bane din sol i det høje,
lyset i sandhed, omrejser vor jord,
intet i verden er skjult for dens øje,
aldrig udslettes dens strålende spor.

Ren som et guld er den lov, du har givet,
omvender sjæle, som agter derpå,
trofast dit vidnesbyrd fører til livet,
vismænd det gør af vankundige små.

(1837)

Lord, of your glory the heavens are telling

Lord, of your glory the heavens are telling,
By the blue welkin the Master is praised,
Sun, moon and stars in their hosts ever swelling
Show us your handiwork, leave us amazed.

But in your house, in your church on earth founded,
There of you every day speaks unto day,
There are your sun and your thunder expounded,
There even night will enlighten our way!

In truth no word or thought ever are given,
Which in your house found their voice and true worth,
And far and wide as the stars roam the heaven
But that they comfort, enlighten on earth.

And with the sun will the word, as times alter,
Come as a bridegroom at first flush of dawn,
Follow its course through the sky without falter,
With sunset's wreath be as hero adorned!

So does God's sun travel on as 'tis bidden,
Light in truth, circling our earth in pure blaze,
Nought here below from its eye can be hidden,
Ne'er shall its radiant track be erased.

Bright as pure gold are the statutes you gave us,
Souls who revere them you never despise,
Your steadfast token to life e'er will save us,
By it are ignorant mortals made wise!

(1837)

Moders navn er en himmelsk lyd

Moders navn er en himmelsk lyd,
så vide som bølgen blåner,
moders røst er den spædes fryd
og glæder, når issen gråner.
Sødt i lyst og sødt i nød,
sødt i liv og sødt i død,
sødt i eftermælet!

Modersmål er det kraftens ord,
som lever i folkemunde,
som det elskes i syd og nord,
så sjunges der sødt i lunde.
Sødt i lyst og sødt i nød,
sødt i liv og sødt i død,
sødt i eftermælet!

Modersmål er det rosenbånd,
som store og små omslynger,
i det lever kun fædres ånd,
og deri kun hjertet gynger.
Sødt i lyst og sødt i nød,
sødt i liv og sødt i død,
sødt i eftermælet!

Modersmål er vort hjertesprog,
kun løs er al fremmed tale,
det alene i mund og bog
kan vække et folk af dvale.
Sødt i lyst og sødt i nød,
sødt i liv og sødt i død,
sødt i eftermælet!

Modersmålet ved Øresund
og trindt i de grønne lunde
dejligt klinger i allen stund,
men dejligst i pigemunde.
Sødt i lyst og sødt i nød,
sødt i liv og sødt i død,
sødt i eftermælet!

(1837)

Mother's name is a heav'nly sound

Mother's name is a heav'nly sound,
as far as blue waves are playing,
mother's voice makes the young heart bound
and cheers all whose hairs are greying.
Sweet in joy and in distress,
sweet in life and sweet in death,
sweet in thought hereafter!

Mother tongue is a living force,
the people's own word completely,
as it's loved both in south and north
in groves it is sung most sweetly.
Sweet in joy and in distress,
sweet in life and sweet in death,
sweet in thought hereafter!

Mother tongue is the twining rose,
that great and small binds together,
ancient spirits but there repose,
and there has the heart its tether.
Sweet in joy and in distress,
sweet in life and sweet in death,
sweet in thought hereafter!

Mother tongue is our heart's true tone,
but chaff those else without number,
it in speech and in book alone
can wake a people from slumber.
Sweet in joy and in distress,
sweet in life and sweet in death,
sweet in thought hereafter!

Mother tongue by the Sound's far shore,
in green groves so fully laden,
sounds delightful as none before,
but most so on lips of maidens.
Sweet in joy and in distress,
sweet in life and sweet in death,
sweet in thought hereafter!

(1837)

Et jævnt og muntert, virksomt liv på jord

Et jævnt og muntert, virksomt liv på jord
som det, jeg ville ej med kongers bytte,
opklaret gang i ædle fædres spor,
med lige værdighed i borg og hytte,
med øjet, som det skabtes, himmelvendt,
lysvågent for alt skønt og stort herneden,
men med de dybe længsler vel bekendt,
kun fyldestgjort af glans fra evigheden;

et sådant liv jeg ønsked al min æt
og pønsed på med flid at forberede,
og når min sjæl blev af sin grublen træt,
den hviled sig ved fadervor at bede.
Da følte jeg den trøst af sandheds ånd,
at lykken svæver over urtegården,
når støvet lægges i sin skabers hånd,
og alting ventes i naturens orden:

Kun spiren frisk og grøn i tidlig vår,
og blomsterfloret i den varme sommer,
da modenhed i møde planten går
og fryder med sin frugt, når høsten kommer!
Om kort, om langt blev løbebanen spændt,
den er til folkegavn, den er til grøde;
som godt begyndt er dagen godt fuldendt,
og lige liflig er dens aftenrøde.

(1839)

A simple, cheerful active life on earth

A simple, cheerful, active life on earth,
A cup I'd not exchange for monarch's chalice,
In noble forebears' tracks a path since birth,
With equal dignity in hut and palace,
With eye as when created heav'nward turned,
All beauty here and grandness keenly knowing,
Familiar though with those things deeply yearned,
Stilled only by eternity's bright glowing.

I wished for all my line just such a life,
And zealously I planned for its fruition,
And when my soul grew tired from toil and strife,
The Lord's Prayer was its rest and its nutrition.
Then from truth's spirit I great comfort gained,
And felt joy hover o'er each garden border,
When dust is placed in its creator's hand
And all is waited for in nature's order:

Just fresh, green buds that sprout in early spring,
And in the summer heat the flowers' profusion;
And when the plants mature and long to bring
Their harvest fruit to autumn's full conclusion!
The human span assigned is short or long,
It is for common weal, its yield is growing;
The day that started well will end as strong,
And just as sweet will be its afterglowing.

(1839)

I al sin glans nu stråler solen

I al sin glans nu stråler solen,
livslyset over nåde-stolen,
nu kom vor pinselilje-tid,
nu har vi sommer skær og blid,
nu spår os mer end englerøst
i Jesu navn en gylden høst.

I sommernattens korte svale
slår højt fredskovens nattergale,
så alt, hvad Herren kalder sit,
må slumre sødt og vågne blidt,
må drømme sødt om Paradis
og vågne til vor Herres pris.

Det ånder himmelsk over støvet,
det vifter hjemligt gennem løvet,
det lufter lifligt under sky
fra Paradis, opladt på ny,
og yndig risler ved vor fod
i engen bæk af livets flod.

Det volder alt den Ånd, som daler,
det virker alt den Ånd, som taler,
ej af sig selv, men os til trøst
af kærlighed med sandheds røst,
i Ordets navn, som her blev kød
og fór til Himmels hvid og rød.

Opvågner, alle dybe toner,
til pris for menneskets forsoner!
Forsamles, alle tungemål,
i takkesangens offerskål!
Istemmer over Herrens bord
nu menighedens fulde kor!

I Jesu navn da tungen gløder
hos hedninger så vel som jøder;
i Jesus-navnets offerskål
hensmelter alle modersmål;
i Jesu navn udbryder da
det evige halleluja.

Vor Gud og Fader uden lige!
Da blomstrer rosen i dit rige,
som sole vi går op og ned
i din Enbårnes herlighed;
thi du for hjertet, vi gav dig,
gav os med ham dit Himmerig.

(1843/1853)

Now gleams the sun in all its splendour

Now gleams the sun in all its splendour,
o'er mercy seat life's light to tender –
now whitsun lily's time is here,
now we have summer mild and clear –
will more than angel's voice proclaim
a golden harvest in Christ's name.

In summer night's brief coolness ringing
the forest's nightingales are singing,
so all that God will ne'er forsake
may sweetly sleep and gently wake,
may sweetly dream of paradise
and wake their God to glorify.

And o'er the dust sighs heav'nly breathing,
and through the leaves wind's gently heaving,
and 'neath the clouds a breeze that blew
from paradise is charged anew,
and in the meadow at our feet
from life's own stream comes murmur sweet.

This wreaks all spirit now descending,
this speaks all spirit without ending
not of itself but – us to soothe –
of love, with voice of lasting truth,
as word made flesh that from the dead
rose up to heaven, white and red!

And all mankind its voice now raises
to sing its great Redeemer's praises!
All tongues together now extol
their Lord at the communion bowl!
Over His table chants entire
the congregation's mighty choir.

In Jesus' name are tongues afire,
as jews and gentiles like aspire,
in Jesus' sacrificial bowl
all tongues now melt to form one whole,
in Jesus' name their voices lend
to Hallelujahs without end!

Our God and Father, mightiest power!
Now blooms the rose in Thy great bower,
like suns do we now rise and set,
in Thy Son's glory are we met,
since for the heart that we gave Thee
through Him Thou gav'st us heaven's key!

(1843/1853)

Velkommen i den grønne lund

Velkommen i den grønne lund,
hvor fuglene de sjunge!
det høres skal: den danske mund
til sang har og en tunge.

Vi har det godt i grunden her,
såvel som vore fædre,
vil Gud, den dag tør være nær,
vi får det end lidt bedre.

Vor konge er vor fuldtro ven,
som guld hans ord må skattes:
"Kom hid, I gode danemænd,
og sig os, hvad I fattes!"

Kan munden vi få ret på gang
til andet end at spise,
hverandet barn i Danevang
forstår halvkvæden vise.

For, hvad vi fattes først og sidst,
til lykke ej så ganske,
men lidt dog både her og hist,
det er det ægte danske.

Derom sang nys en lille fugl
i syd på Skamlingsbanke,
og synd det var at lægge skjul
på hele folkets tanke.

Vi føre løver i vort skjold
af hjerter tæt omsatte,
dem førte vi fra hedenold
og ingen abekatte.

Hver fugl må synge med sit næb,
og livet, kan vi skønne,
var uden sang kun slid og slæb.
Velkommen i det grønne!

(1843)

Thrice welcome to the leafy grove

Thrice welcome to the leafy grove,
where birds are sweetly singing!
Let too the Danish tongue now prove
its song can set things ringing.

For all in all we're well off here,
like those of old who bore us
God willing, may the day be near
when more still lies before us.

Our king, a trusty friend is he,
his words like gold we treasure:
'Come hither, good Danes, tell to me
where you've been served short measure!'

If we could all our mouths command
to more besides just eating,
Each second child in Denmark's land
would grasp what won't need speaking.

Not much is needed joy to share
and present lacks to banish,
a little though, both here and there,
that's what is truly Danish.

On Skamling hill the other day
a little bird sang clearly,
and 'twould be shame to hide away
the thoughts that all felt dearly.

Proud lions adorn the Danish shield
bestrewn with hearts unshrinking,
since days of old they hold the field,
not miming apes unthinking.

Each bird its special song must find,
for life would without singing
be merely drudgery and grind.
So welcome, hear it ringing!

(1843)

At sige verden ret farvel

At sige verden ret farvel
i livets gry og livets kvæld
er lige tungt at nemme;
det lærtes aldrig her på jord,
var, Jesus, ej du i dit ord
hos os, som du er hjemme.

Hvor tit hos dig end trøst jeg fandt,
når hjertet skjalv, og gråden randt,
og verdens bølger bruste,
ved støvet hænger dog min sjæl,
og slangen bider i min hæl,
skønt du dens hoved knuste.

O Jesus, Herre, broder sød!
Du kender bedst den bitre død,
du har den overvundet;
vor skabning grant og kender du,
ved godt, vi alle ser med gru
vort timeglas udrundet.

O, kom du, som engang, jeg ved,
du i din Faders herlighed
skal klart dig åbenbare,
var det i gry, var det i kvæld,
jeg skyndte mig med kort farvel
i sky til dig at fare.

Men kommer døden førend du,
kom da i løn, og kom i hu,
hvor mørkt der er i graven!
Omstrål mig, så jeg glemmer den,
salv øjet på din syge ven,
så jeg kan se Guds-haven!

Kom i den sidste nattevagt
i en af mine kæres dragt,
og sæt dig ved min side,
og tal med mig, som ven med ven,
om, hvor vi snart skal ses igen
og glemme al vor kvide!

Kom, som du vil! jeg ved det vist,
du selv har sagt, at her og hist
du kendes vil på røsten,
den røst, hvorved trods verdens larm
os hjertet brænde kan i barm
og smelte hen i trøsten.

O, lad mig i min sidste stund
det høre af din egen mund,
som Ånd og liv kan tale,
hvor godt der er i Himmerig,
og at du stol har sat til mig
i dine lyse sale!

Før døden med sin istap-hånd
gør skel imellem støv og ånd,
bortvifter hjertets varme,
indslumre skal jeg da med lyst,
som barnet ved sin moders bryst,
i dine frelserarme.

(1843/1845)

To rightly bid the world farewell

To rightly bid the world farewell
at life's first dawn or evening knell
is hard for us to fathom.
It never would be learnt on earth,
were you not with us in your word,
Oh Jesus, as in heaven.

Though solace oft I found with you,
when my heart quaked, and tears broke through,
and worldly waves did thunder,
my soul to dust yet seeks to cling,
my heel the serpent yet does sting,
though you its head did sunder.

Oh Jesus, Master, brother sweet!
Death's bitterness you know complete,
for you all death did vanquish.
You know us fully, every one,
know well, time's sands that ever run
our hearts do fill with anguish.

Oh come, as once you did, I know
you will yourself quite clearly show
in all your Father's glory,
were it at dawn or evening knell,
I'd rise up with but brief farewell
your heav'nly cloud before me.

But should death come before you do,
come secretly, remember too
the grave will all things darken!
Enhalo me, that darkness end,
anoint the eye of your sick friend,
so I may see God's garden!

In the last night watch, come, draw near,
arrayed in clothes of one who's dear
and sit down close beside me,
and speak with me, as friend to friend,
of where we soon will meet again,
forget what pains us direly!

Come as you wish! For well I know
you've said your voice may here below
reveal you to creation:
that voice, though all the world should rage,
which makes our heart within us blaze
and melt in consolation.

Oh, let me at my final hour
hear from your mouth that with great power
can speak of life and spirit:
how heaven beckons constantly,
how in your halls a chair for me
awaits which I'll inherit!

Ere death with icy hand should strive
'twixt dust and spirit to divide,
and make heart's warmth grow dimmer,
with trusting eagerness I'll rest,
as does the child at mother's breast,
embraced by my redeemer.

(1843/1845)

Er lyset for de lærde blot

Er lyset for de lærde blot
til ret og galt at stave?
Nej, himlen under flere godt,
og lys er himlens gave,
og solen står med bonden op,
slet ikke med de lærde,
oplyser bedst fra tå til top,
hvem der er mest på færde.

Er lyset i planeter kun,
som ej kan se og mæle?
Er ikke ordet i vor mund
et lys for alle sjæle?
Det giver os for ånder syn,
som solens skin for kroppe,
det slår i sjælen ned som lyn
fra skyerne hist oppe.

Er lys på visse vilkår blot
så halvvejs at ophøje?
Gør det ej alle vegne godt
er lys ej livets øje!
Skal for misbrugens skyld måske
på åndens himmelbue
vi heller mulm og mørke se
end solens blanke lue?

Nej, aldrig spørges det fra Nord,
vi lyset vil fordunkle!
Som nordlys i fribårne ord
det sås på himlen funkle,
og ses det skal ved nordens pol,
ej blot i kroppens rige:
midsommerens den bolde sol
vil ej for midnat vige!

Oplysning være skal vor lyst,
er det så kun om sivet,
men først og sidst med folkerøst
oplysningen om livet;
den springer ud af folkedåd
og vokser, som den vugges,
den stråle i vort folkeråd,
til aftenstjernen slukkes!

(1844)

Is light but for the learned few

Is light but for the learned few
to try and spell unstriven?
No, heav'n would bless all others too
and light's a gift from heaven,
the sun will with the farmer go
the learned few eschewing,
it best lights up from top to toe
the one who's up and doing.

Is light the planets' sole domain
no sight and speech possessing?
Is not the word our mouth can frame
a light where souls find blessing!
Thereby all spirits we behold,
as sun's rays bodies brighten,
it strikes like lightning in the soul
and does from clouds enlighten.

Does light on certain terms alone
deserve our praise so poorly?
Is light not everywhere a boon!
For it is life's eye surely!
Shall we because of errant ways
in spirit's vault of heaven
on pitch-black darkness rather gaze
than on sun's blazing beacon?

No, from the North was never heard
that light we would be dimming!
like northern lights in free-born word
'twas seen in heaven gleaming,
and shall at northern pole be seen
not only here 'mongst mortals;
midsummer's valiant sun's bright sheen
defies black midnight's portals!

Enlightenment shall be our joy,
though reeds alone be brightened,
but first and last with common voice
may all life be enlightened;
it has its source in common deed
and grows as it is tended,
may it our common council feed
till evening star is ended!

(1844)

Nu falmer skoven trindt om land

Nu falmer skoven trindt om land,
og fuglestemmen daler;
alt flygted storken over strand,
ham følger viltre svaler.

Hvor marken bølged nys som guld
med aks og vipper bolde,
der ser man nu kun sorten muld
og stubbene de golde.

Men i vor lade, på vor lo,
der har vi nu Guds gaver,
der virksomhed og velstand gro
i tøndemål af traver.

Og han, som vokse lod på jord
de gyldne aks og vipper,
han bliver hos os med sit ord,
det ord, som aldrig glipper.

Ham takker alle vi med sang
for alt, hvad han har givet,
for hvad han vokse lod i vang,
for ordet og for livet.

Da over os det hele år
sin fred han lyser gerne,
og efter vinter kommer vår
med sommer, korn og kerne.

Og når engang på Herrens bud
vort timeglas udrinder,
en evig sommer hos vor Gud
i Paradis vi finder.

Da høste vi, som fugle nu,
der ikke så og pløje;
da komme aldrig mer i hu
vi jordens strid og møje.

For høsten her og høsten hist
vor Gud ske lov og ære,
som ved vor Herre Jesus Krist
vor Fader ville være!

Hans Ånd, som alting kan og ved,
i disse korte dage
med tro og håb og kærlighed
til Himlen os ledsage!

(1844)

Now every wood grows pale and wan

Now every wood grows pale and wan
and voice of bird soon parting,
the stork has crossed the shore and gone –
pursued by swallows darting.

Where fields but recently like gold
with ears of corn were swaying,
is only soil that's black and cold
with stubble old and greying.

But threshing floor and barn are now
where we God's gifts have treasured,
where active toil and wealth will grow
from stooks in bushels measured.

And he who out of earthly clay
let golden corn be scaling
is with us with his word alway,
the word that's never-failing.

Him do we thank with songs of praise
for all that he's been giving:
for summer cornfields all ablaze,
his word, and life for living!

Then over us throughout the year
he lets his peace shine gently,
and, winter over, spring is here
with summer, corn and plenty.

And when at last at his command
from earth we must be wending,
with God in paradise we'll stand
in summer never-ending.

Then we shall reap as birds do now
though theirs was not the sowing,
then we shall ne'er remember how
earth's toil and strife kept growing.

For harvest there and harvest here
to God all praise and glory,
who by our Lord, Christ Jesus dear
would be our Father surely.

May then his mighty spirit move
and us, in days fast waning,
raise up through faith and hope and love
till paradise attaining!

(1844)

Skyerne gråner, og løvet falder

Skyerne gråner, og løvet falder,
fuglene synger ej mer,
vinteren truer, og natten kalder,
blomsterne sukker: det sner!
Og dog bære blus vi med glæde!

Vinteren kommer, og sneen falder,
blomsterne visner i muld,
isen optøs ej af gråd for Balder,
tårerne stivner af kuld.
Og dog bære blus vi med glæde!

Solhvervet kommer, og bladet vendes,
dagene længes på ny,
solskinnet vokser, og vintren endes,
lærkerne synger i sky.
Derfor bære blus vi med glæde!

Årene skifter af gru for ælde,
skjaldene giver dem ret,
fuglene alle hvert år må fælde,
ellers de fløj ej så let:
Derfor bære blus vi med glæde!

Fuglene flyver som vind på vinger
let over vildene hav,
skjaldene flyver, som rimet klinger,
glat over slægternes grav.
Derfor bære blus vi med glæde!

Hjerterne vakler, når højt de banke,
drages til fuglenes spor,
lyset dog sejrer, den mørke tanke
flygtende synker i jord.
Derfor bære blus vi med glæde!

Salmerne klinge og klokker kime,
spotter med sneen ved jul,
vinteren må sig med våren rime,
smelte for solen i skjul.
Derfor bære blus vi med glæde!

Troende hjerter i vinterløbet
føder den liflige vår,
trykker den til sig i barnesvøbet
med et lyksaligt nytår!
Derfor bære blus vi med glæde!

Bethlehems-barnet i krybberummet
det er den evige vår,
troende hjerter det har fornummet:
Jul gør lyksaligt nytår!
Derfor bære blus vi med glæde!

(1847)

Grey grow the clouds

Grey grow the clouds and the leaves are falling,
hushed are the birds long ago,
winter now threatens, and night is calling
flowers sadly sigh: see the snow!
And yet we the torch gladly carry!

Winter is coming, and snow is falling,
flowers wilt and die in their mould,
weeping for Balder no ice is thawing
stiff grow all tears from the cold.
And yet we the torch gladly carry!

Solstice draws near, a new page is turning,
days start to lengthen once more,
sunshine increases, the winter spurning,
larks sing as skyward they soar.
Therefore we the torch gladly carry!

Fearing old age, years replace each other
as every bard knows is right,
birds every year have to shed their feathers
to add more lift to their flight.
Therefore we the torch gladly carry!

Birds fly as swift as the wind when winging
lightly o'er wildest of waves,
bards fly aloft, with their rhymes full-ringing,
smoothly o'er ancestors' graves.
Therefore we the torch gladly carry!

Hearts start to falter when loudly beating,
drawn to the birds' parting track,
light though now triumphs, dark thoughts defeating,
into the ground drives them back
Therefore we the torch gladly carry!

Hymns ring out gladly, and bells are chiming,
as Christmas snow they deride,
winter with springtime must needs be rhyming,
melts though the sun has to hide.
Therefore we the torch gladly carry!

Hearts full of faith midst the winter's sadness
give birth to spring bright and clear,
press close the babe newly born with gladness
sure of a blessed New Year!
Therefore we the torch gladly carry!

Bethlehem's child in the manger lowly
means spring eternal is here,
hearts full of faith sense the message holy:
Christmas will bless the New Year!
Therefore we the torch gladly carry!

(1847)

Jeg gik mig ud en sommerdag at høre

Jeg gik mig ud en sommerdag at høre
fuglesang, som hjertet kunne røre,
i de dybe dale,
mellem nattergale
og de andre fugle små, som tale.

Der sad en lille fugl i bøgelunden,
sødt den sang i sommer-aftenstunden,
i de grønne sale,
mellem nattergale
og de andre fugle små, som tale.

Den sang så sødt om dejligst vang og vænge,
hvor kærminder gro, som græs i enge.

Den sang om alt, hvad det er lyst at høre,
allerhelst, hvad hjertet dybt kan røre.

Den sang, som ingen andre fugle sjunge,
leged liflig med min moders tunge.

Den sang som talt ud af mit eget hjerte,
toner gav den al min fryd og smerte.

Da nynned jeg så småt i aftenstunden:
Flyv, Guldtop, flyv rundt i bøgelunden.

O, flyv fra Øresund til Danevirke!
syng til dans, til skole og til kirke.

På folkets modersmål, med Danmarks tunge,
syng, som ingen andre fugle sjunge.

Da mærke alle, som har mødre kære,
det er godt i Danmark at være.

Da gløder alt, hvad solen har bestrålet,
som det røde guld på modersmålet.
i de dybe dale,
mellem nattergale
og de andre fugle små som tale.

(1847)

I walked abroad one summer's day

I walked abroad one summer's day to hear
song of bird that through my heart might sear,
in the deep, green dales,
midst the nightingales
and each bird that now my heart regales.

A little bird sat in the beech-tree grove,
sweet it sang in summer's twilight mauve,
in the leafy vales,
midst the nightingales
and each bird that now my heart regales.

It sang so sweet of meadows lush and low,
where like grass forgetmenots do grow.

It sang of everything one fain would hear,
most of all what through the heart can sear,

It sang as no bird else has ever sung,
played so grandly with my mother tongue,

It sang as if my heart itself did speak,
pain and joy were notes from its small beak,

And then I murmured in the twilight mauve:
Fly, Gold Crest! fly round your beech-tree grove,

Oh, fly from north to south, from west to east,
sing at Danish school, church, dance and feast,

In common Danish, in our mother tongue,
sing aloud like no bird else has sung,

Then all who hold their mothers dear will know
Denmark is a place where hearts can grow,

Then all will gleam that's lit up by the sun,
like red gold upon our mother tongue,
in the deep, green dales,
midst the nightingales
and each bird that now my heart regales.

(1847)

Midsommers-Natten ved Frederiksborg

Kølig det lufter i måneskin mat,
blomsterne dufter i midsommer nat,
og borgen i søen på Hillerødsøen
står gammel og grå, mens fuglene slå
i nattergals lunden hin fejre.

Kølig det lufter i måneskin mat,
blomsterne dufter i midsommers nat,
men gråhærdet kæmpe i Danemarks Tempe
sig hviler så blødt og blunder så sødt
som nattergalsungen i lunden.

Kølig det lufter i alderdoms år,
høsten ej dufter lig sommer og vår;
men prisen dog vinder med aks og kærminder
den grundrige høst fra vårtidens lyst
i nattergalslunden hin fejre.

(1849)

Midsummer Night at Frederiksborg

Cool winds sigh softly in moon's dimmish light,
flower scent is wafting this midsummer's night,
the grey castle, lake-bound on Hillerød island,
stands ancient and still, while birds softly trill
in fair groves with nightingales calling.

Cool winds sigh softly in moon's dimmish light,
flower scent is wafting this midsummer's night,
the warrior's last embers in Denmark's own Tempe
find long yearned-for rest, with sleep he is blessed
like nightingale fledgling in hedgerow.

Cool winds sigh softly though old age now clings,
autumn's scent wafts less than summer's and spring's,
but greater its power, with corn, blue-eyed flower
a harvest entire of spring's keen desire
in fair groves with nightingales calling.

(1849)

Alt, hvad som fuglevinger fik

Alt, hvad som fuglevinger fik,
alt, hvad som efter fugleskik
med sanglyd drager ånde,
lovsynge Gud, for han er god,
han i sin nåde råder bod
på støvets ve og vånde.

Min sjæl, du har af alt på jord
i tanken og din tunges ord
de allerbedste vinger,
og friest er dit åndefang,
når dybt du drager det i sang,
så højt i sky det klinger.

Hvad er vel og på jorderig,
der sammenlignes kan med dig
i trangen til Guds nåde?
Og det var dig, den ledte om,
da med vor Herre hid den kom
på underligste måde.

Så vågn da op, min sjæl, bryd ud
med lovsangs røst, og pris din Gud,
din skaber og genløser,
som så til dig i nåde ned
og over os sin kærlighed
med Trøsteren udøser!

Og sig det til hver fugl på jord,
og sig til alle englekor,
hvis sang livsaligst klinger,
at du med dem i væddestrid
vil prise Gud til evig tid
for ånde, røst og vinger!

(1851)

All birds that God gave wings to fly

All birds that God gave wings to fly,
all things that as the birds do cry
and sing while breath they're drawing,
now praise their God, for good He is,
and in His mercy remedies
life's pangs and painful gnawing.

My soul, of all that is on earth,
of what in thought and tongue has birth,
most strongly you are winging,
and freest is the breath you take
when out of it a hymn you make
that sends the heavens ringing.

What is there on this earth so true
that can be likened unto you
that would God's grace be craving?
And it was you for which it sought
when with our Lord 'twas hither brought
all earthly ways outbraving.

Then wake, my soul, your voice now raise,
with joyful songs your Master praise,
that did redeem creation,
that when in mercy you He saw,
He over us His love did pour,
His comfort and salvation.

And tell each bird on earth anew,
and tell all choirs of angels too,
whose song full sweet is ringing,
that you with them will gladly vie,
will ever praise the Lord most high
for breath, for wings and singing!

(1851)

Morgenstund har guld i mund

Morgenstund
har guld i mund;
for natten Gud vi love;
han lærte os, i Jesu navn,
som barnet i sin moders favn
vi alle sødt kan sove.

Morgenstund
har guld i mund;
vi til vort arbejd ile,
som fuglen glad i skov og vang
udflyver med sin morgensang,
genfødt ved nattehvile.

Morgenstund
har guld i mund,
og guld betyder glæde,
og glædelig er hver en dag,
som leves til Guds velbehag,
om end vi måtte græde.

Gå da frit
enhver til sit
og stole på Guds nåde!
Da får vi lyst og lykke til
at gøre gavn, som Gud det vil,
på allerbedste måde.

Sol opstår,
og sol nedgår,
når den har gjort sin gerning;
Gud give os at skinne så,
som himmellys, skønt af de små!
Da randt for os guldterning.

(1853)

Golden dawn sees us reborn

Golden dawn
sees us reborn;
we praise God for night's keeping;
he taught us all, through Jesus' grace,
as child in mother's warm embrace,
sweet rest when safely sleeping.

Golden dawn
sees us reborn;
to daily work we hasten,
as birds in wood and meadow fly
with joyful song into the sky,
from night's reincarnation.

Golden dawn
sees us reborn,
and gold means joy and gladness,
and glad is he who every day
would please his God in every way,
e'en when oppressed by sadness.

Freely make
the path to take
on God's great grace relying!
Then will our wish and fortune be
to do what's fruitful constantly,
God's wishes sanctifying.

Morning sun,
its course full run
at evening has its setting;
God grant that we may shine as bright,
as heav'nly light, though we be slight!
Us golden joy begetting.

(1853)

Det er så yndigt at følges ad

Det er så yndigt at følges ad
for to, som gerne vil sammen være;
da er med glæden man dobbelt glad
og halvt om sorgen så tung at bære;
ja, det er gammen
:|: at rejse sammen,:|:
når fjederhammen
:|: er kærlighed.:|:

Det er så hyggeligt allensteds,
hvor små og store har ét i sinde,
og det, som drager de store læs,
i hjertekamret er inderst inde;
ja, det er gammen
:|: at holde sammen,:|:
når ja og amen
:|: er hjertets sprog.:|:

Det er så herligt at stole på,
vi har en Herre, som alting mægter,
han os ej glemmer, når vi er grå,
hans nåde rækker til tusind slægter;
ja, det er gammen,
:|: at alle sammen:|:
er ja og amen
:|: Guds nådes ord.:|:

Det er vemodigt at skilles ad,
for dem, som gerne vil sammen være,
men, Gud ske lov! i vor Herres stad
for evig samles de hjertenskære;
ja, det er gammen
:|: at leve sammen,:|:
hvor ja og amen
:|: er kærlighed.:|:

Hvert ægtepar, som med kærlighed
i Jesu navn holder bryllupsgilde,
skønt alt i verden går op og ned,
skal finde tidlig og finde silde:
Det er dog gammen
:|: at sidde sammen,:|:
hvor arneflammen
:|: er kærlighed.:|:

(1855)

It's so delightful to be as one

It's so delightful to be as one,
For two who dearly life would be sharing,
Each joy is felt to be doubly won,
Each sorrow's burden is half the bearing;
Yes, it's fair weather
:|: To walk together,:|:
Two birds, one feather,
:|: In love, true love!:|:

It's so agreeable everywhere
Where great and small the same mind are sharing,
And those great loads which we all must bear
Are lessened by the heart's tender caring;
Yes, it's fair weather
:|: To stay together,:|:
When now and ever
:|: Is heart's true voice.:|:

It's so inspiring to know each day
We have a Master of all life's stations,
He'll not forsake us when we are grey,
His mercy lasts to all generations;
Yes, it's fair weather,
:|: That altogether:|:
Both now and ever
:|: Is God's true word!:|:

It's so distressing to have to part
For those who dearly life would be sharing,
But God be praised! All those dear of heart
Re-meet in heaven to joy unsparing;
Yes, it's fair weather
:|: To live together,:|:
When now and ever
:|: Is love, true love!:|:

Each wedding couple who pledge their vow
In Jesus' name, and in fullest measure,
Though earthly fortune be high or low,
Will find both early and late life's treasure:
For it's fair weather
:|: To sit together,:|:
When fired for ever
:|: By love, true love.:|:

(1855)

Kimer, I klokker!

Kimer, I klokker! ja, kimer før dag i det dunkle!
Tindrer, I stjerner, som englenes øjne kan funkle!
Fred kom til jord,
Himmelens fred med Guds Ord.
Æren er Guds i det høje!

Julen er kommet med solhverv for hjerterne bange,
jul med Guds-barnet i svøb, under englenes sange,
kommer fra Gud,
bringer os glædskabens bud.
Æren er Guds i det høje!

Synger og danser, og klapper i eders småhænder,
menneskebørnene alle til jorderigs ender!
Født er i dag
barnet til Guds velbehag.
Æren er Guds i det høje!

(1856)

Ring out, ye bells

Ring out, ye bells, yes, ring out ere night starts to lighten!
Sparkle, ye stars, so your gleam may all angels' eyes brighten!
Peace came to earth,
Heavenly peace with God's word.
Glory to God in the highest!

Christmas is come, sun's return to faint hearts it is bringing,
Christmas with God's swaddled babe while the angels are singing,
comes from above,
joyful its message of love.
Glory to God in the highest!

Clap your hands, dance, all ye children of God, raise your voices,
To the far ends of the world now each mortal rejoices!
Born is this night
He who is God's great delight.
Glory to God in the highest!

(1856)

Hvad solskin er for det sorte muld

Hvad solskin er for det sorte muld,
er sand oplysning for muldets frænde;
langt mere værd end det røde guld
det er sin Gud og sig selv at kende;
trods mørkets harme,
i strålearme
af lys og varme
er lykken klar!

Som solen skinner i forårstid,
og som den varmer i sommerdage,
al sand oplysning er mild og blid,
så den vort hjerte må vel behage;
trods mørkets harme,
i strålearme
af lys og varme
er hjertensfryd!

Som urter blomstre og kornet gror
i varme dage og lyse nætter,
så livs-oplysning i høje Nord
vor ungdom blomster og frugt forjætter;
trods mørkets harme,
i strålearme
af lys og varme
er frugtbarhed!

Som fuglesangen i grønne lund,
der liflig klinger i vår og sommer,
vort modersmål i vor ungdoms mund
skal liflig klinge, når lyset kommer;
trods mørkets harme,
i strålearme
af lys og varme
er røsten klar!

Vorherre vidner, at lys er godt,
som sandhed elskes, så lyset yndes,
og med Vorherre, som ler ad spot,
skal værket lykkes, som her begyndes;
trods mørkets harme,
i strålearme
af lys og varme
vor skole stå!

(1856)

What sunshine is for the rich black earth

What sunshine is for the rich black earth,
is true enlightenment for earth's kinsmen.
Red gold is too of far lesser worth
than knowing God and what's deep within one.
Though darkness storms us
in bright arms glorious
that light and warm us
our joy shines clear!

As gleams the sun, when by spring beguiled,
and in the summer sends warmth that's healing,
all true enlightenment's meek and mild,
so each heart's drawn by its force appealing.
Though darkness storms us
in bright arms glorious
that light and warm us
is heartfelt bliss!

Like plants all flower and the young corn climbs
in long, warm days when the night seems farthest,
our youth, enlightened in northern climes,
will flower and promise a rich life-harvest.
Though darkness storms us
in bright arms glorious
that light and warm us
will all bear fruit!

Like birdsong deep in the leafy grove
that rings out sweetly in spring and summer,
the mother tongue that our youth's lips moves
will ring out sweetly when light's forthcoming.
Though darkness storms us
in bright arms glorious
that light and warm us
the voice sounds clear!

Our Lord God praises the light that burns,
as truth is loved, so is light's ambition,
and with Our Lord, who all scoffing spurns,
the work begun here will gain fruition.
Though darkness storms us
in bright arms glorious
that light and warm us
may our school stand!

(1856)

Danish Titles

Alt, hvad som fuglevinger fik 72
At sige verden ret farvel 60
Dejlig er den himmel blå 22
Den signede dag med fryd vi ser 34
Det er så yndigt at følges ad 76
Er lyset for de lærde blot 62
Et jævnt og muntert, virksomt liv på jord 54
Forunderligt at sige 48
Giv mig, Gud, en salmetunge 40
Har hånd du lagt på Herrens plov 42
Hil dig, Frelser og Forsoner 46
Himlene, Herre, fortælle din ære 50
Hvad solskin er for det sorte muld 80
I al sin glans nu stråler solen 56
Jeg gik mig ud en sommerdag at høre 68
Jeg kender et land 30
Kimer, I klokker! 78
Kirken den er et gammelt hus 44
Langt højere bjerge så vide på jord 28
Midsommers-Natten ved Frederiksborg 70
Moders navn er en himmelsk lyd 52
Morgenhanen atter gol 38
Morgenstund har guld i mund 74
Nu falmer skoven trindt om land 64
Påskeblomst! hvad vil du her? 24
Skyerne gråner, og løvet falder 66
Velkommen i den grønne lund 58

English Titles

All birds that God gave wings to fly 73
A simple, cheerful active life on earth 55
Easter flower! what would you here? 25
Far higher are mountains in other lands found 29
Golden dawn sees us reborn 75
Grant me, God, a tongue to praise you 41
Grey grow the clouds 67
Hail, you Saviour and Redeemer 47
If once the Lord's plough you hold sure 43
I know of a land 31
Is light but for the learned few 63
It is a wondrous story 49
It's so delightful to be as one 77
I walked abroad one summer's day 69
Lord, of your glory the heavens are telling 51
Lovely is the sky of blue 23
Midsummer Night at Frederiksborg 71
Mother's name is a heav'nly sound 53
Now every wood grows pale and wan 65
Now gleams the sun in all its splendour 57
Once more did the dawn cock crow 39
Ring out, ye bells 79
The bright blessed day with joy we see 35
The church, that ancient house, will stand 45
Thrice welcome to the leafy grove 59
To rightly bid the world farewell 61
What sunshine is for the rich black earth 81